MW00413267

THE
SPECULATOR'S
MOSAIC

ROBERT LEPPO

The Speculator's Mosaic

Robert Leppo

Printed in the United States of America

First Printing, 2019

ISBN 978-1-08-000743-1

Contents

Foreword

For a moment, imagine an eager young entrepreneur, investor, speculator, or even poker player. Imagine the energy and exuberance he or she experiences with their youth. Next, imagine yourself as an experienced and humbled human who has successfully navigated all the challenges by experiencing every dead end possible.

From the position of this wisdom, could you predict some of the dead ends that this eager young person will go through? For those of us who are older, the answer is unquestionably yes. For those who may be younger, you may understand theoretically that there will be many challenges and dead ends. And, if you are fully aware, you will realize that you don't know what you don't know.

If you are dedicated to success in any one of these fields, you likely read a lot of books about what you should do to achieve success, many written by individuals who have reached the pinnacle in their field. You are told the outcomes you should seek and perhaps even strategies to follow to achieve those outcomes.

However, something is missing. Not a little something – a big something. As Kevin Kline's character, Otto, asked in the movie *A Fish Called Wanda*, "What is the middle thing?"

Yes, indeed, what is the middle thing!

This book, *The Speculator's Mosaic*, is all about that "middle thing" – that is, the internal journey we take, the mistakes we make, the course corrections that create the mindset, and the strategies that give us an edge over the competition.

Author Robert Leppo is able to deliver on the "middle thing" for the following reasons:

1. He is comfortable in his own skin.
2. He experiences a minimal level of both "shame" and "blame."

3.   He is aware of his internal processes.
4.   He accepts what he discovers.
5.   He learns and lets go of what doesn't work.
6.   He is able to clearly articulate his internal process.
7.   He is able to refine his strategies as a learner who is curious about his world.
8.   He continually challenges himself.
9.   He is transparent and honest with us.

As a result, he's given us readers a gift. We can viscerally feel the journey we are embarking on. I can personally identify with the experiences in each of his stories. This is so important because our intellectual understanding can so easily be sabotaged by our emotions and biases. Bob has identified the emotions and biases that have hurt him and helped him. Not only has he identified them, but he tells us how he uses his emotions, such as fear and greed, in real time to help move him towards a better decision-making process. Each point emerges out of a real life story that is engaging and informative.

Reading Bob's real life story can have a greater impact than merely learning more investor strategies. In my work as a coach to speculators, investors, and professional money managers, I see many who have become "stuck" with a mental model of how the world works. From the "stuckness" they shape the incoming information by deleting relevant parts, distorting what they see, and nominalizing dynamic, complex systems into more easily managed fixed concepts. The danger, of course, is that these filters are created to fit their biases.

These investors, traders, and speculators are driven to invest and trade with a decision-making process that was created to fill an internal need and bias rather than by seeing the market and its dynamics as they are. For example, I have portfolio managers who are more driven by competing with their peers than by waiting for opportunities. They are driven more by creating outcomes than by improving their process. As a result, they get caught chasing outcomes. When they get lucky, they're happy. When they miss their numbers, they try harder to attain the self-defined outcome without improving their internal state of mind and how they operate in the world. This creates pressure on the money managers to double down on a failed process.

Bob is all about improving his process. This is the "middle thing." Rather than double down on what isn't working, Bob learns and grows. He actively looks to shed his biases. He's developed an internal mindset and process that removes the stress that most speculators and money managers experience. He has replaced stressful outcomes with curiosity and delight. He has honed a process that works for him – and can work for all of us.

I want to encourage all readers of this book, not to strive for the exact same investment strategy that Bob has created for himself, but to model his resilience and learning method to build a process that is uniquely yours – one that feels good to you, honors your values, and, in the long run, produces the results you want. Focus on the process, not the outcome.

I have known Bob for more years than I can remember. Through those years, I've always been amazed with how easily he seems to handle his decision to make a new investment. I look at the risk and it takes my breath away. But Bob has honed his decision-making process. What looks like incredible risk to me is actually a refined process. This process for angel investing is worth the entire book alone. I recently watched Bob manage the process of considering an investment in a company I introduced him to. True to his process, he found creative ways to bridge the gap between what the company was looking for and a critical piece he could provide.

Even more important, he was having fun!

There's an old joke about being a contrarian: "Contrarian investors buy when others want to sell. A real contrarian buys when he wants to sell." Bob enlarges on a number of contrarian trades he made. What's amazing about this man is that he persists regardless of losses. They don't discourage him, they simply refine his process.

As a coach and trainer for traders and investors, I've learned from neuroscience research that our brain chemistry changes with a series of successes or losses. Bob is more immune from this brain chemistry shift through a process of managing his emotional state. As a result, he has picked himself up, dusted himself off, and started thinking creatively *without* putting an anchor on his optimism. He has done this not once, not twice, but multiple times.

This doesn't mean he shuns success. One critical factor I've learned from Bob's process is that he fully expects those "big paydays." He's curious as to how they'll happen, constantly massaging his investments with that expectation in mind. Although it seems counterintuitive, some of my clients become so immersed in the struggle to achieve success that the struggle itself becomes their world. In this book, you'll watch Bob as he moves from a world of "struggle" to a world where the big "paydays" are a natural part of the process, a constant of the equation.

Here is the genius of this book: because his stories are so revealing, you can follow his thought process and incorporate it into your own experience. Many books create a gap between the "success" and our current state. Bob fills this gap. He concentrates on the "middle thing," improving his process. With this understanding, along with how he views the markets, new ventures, and poker, you can skip many of the dead ends that most of us have traveled down.

This is indeed the middle thing we all sorely need.

Richard Friesen
Founder and CEO, Mind Muscles Academy

Introduction

Gambling is one of the broad activities of life in which individuals differ widely. Many shy away from gambling because of the risk of loss, while others welcome the chance to gamble. In my case, I dove into gambling – or, as the concept appears in this book, speculation. Why? Because I was from an early age sucked into another broad activity about which people differ: reading. Even the first area of speculation I engaged in – poker – was illuminated by books on poker.

So it's no surprise that I have chosen to write *The Speculator's Mosaic* about my own journey of speculation. After all, in large part, I think I have something of value to say because I've supported myself through successful (i.e., profitable) speculation. More important, I have something unique to say (in the sense that it's covered by no other book) about the process of engaging in profitable speculation.

Most of my success and effort has been in three areas of financial speculation: the US stock market, the commodity futures market, and the start-up venture capital market.

In each of these three markets, the reader will learn specifics of the successful tactics I've developed. In many cases, those tactics did not come early or easily due to the wealth of mistakes I made along the way. Those mistakes were largely caused by a combination of laziness, stubbornness, and a world-class ability to rationalize why I did not need to master three key areas of successful investing – emotion, illusion, and cycles. But there is a resonance of satisfaction once you realize you can learn from mistakes and find opportunities that most people lack the means to uncover.

I don't claim that my tactics for successful speculation are the only ones that work. But I do believe that the benefit I derived from speculation came only because I combined tactics that work with tactics that fit my personality. Consult my friend Rich Friesen's fine foreword for more on this point.

Since I played my first hand of poker, the way investors approach speculation has continually morphed. Just since my formative years, we've witnessed the rise and fall of conglomerates, the Nifty Fifty, inflation, stagflation, the advent of supply-side economics, junk bond hysteria, the Go-Go '90s, emerging market mania, and the subprime mortgage meltdown. At the same time, we've seen a cycle of speculation methods, including value investing, growth investing, passive investing, and the rise of the quant.

For many, investing has turned into little more than an abstraction, driven by adaptive software, big data, and MIT PhD graduates. Speculation once involved a deep understanding of market forces and market players. Today, though, algorithms do more and more of the trading, often at close to light speed.

But even with today's ascendant technology, there's still something deeply human about the markets. People still set the prices. They pull the levers and push the buttons that make the computers hum. They write the columns or appear on the TV shows that spread hype, fan the flames of FUD, and overvalue assets; that drive bubbles and crash markets. It wasn't a software glitch, after all, that caused the Great Recession of 2008. It was human greed bordering on delusion.

Because of these realities, it could be argued that there's nothing fundamentally new in speculation.

The risks are still great, and the rewards even greater. If you understand yourself – and understand the person or people on the other side of the trade – you can make a fortune. These are the lessons of *The Reminiscences of a Stock Operator* by Edwin Lefevre and *The Money Game* by Adam Smith, two of the perennial classics of investing. The fact that both of these books are still in print and still inspire billionaire traders like Paul Tudor Jones and Ken Fisher reveals a clear truth: everything that was said before about the markets still applies to the markets of today. And since our emotions don't change – we all feel fear, greed, happiness, elation, sorrow, dejection, and apathy – the same will hold in the future.

Yet, any number of investment professionals and investment books will tell you the *art* of speculation should be seen more and more as the *science* of speculation: cold, calculated, and predictable. That investments should be made solely on basis of charts, data, analytics, and spec sheets. That successfully balancing opportunity and risk can be wrapped up in a simple formula or can't-miss scheme, in mathematical constants and fixed ratios.

In contrast, *The Speculator's Mosaic* focuses on the uniquely human market movers: roiling emotion, psychologically driven cycles, and the power of illusion. Patterned after the classic works by Lefevre and Smith, this book explores the messy pieces of the investment game, then shows readers how to assemble those pieces into a clear picture of the markets.

This picture is, as I call it, the speculator's mosaic.

THE GOOD AND THE BAD

A resource for anyone looking to take up speculation as a profession (or even as a "side hustle"), *The Speculator's Mosaic* lays bare my tried-and-true experience of making, and sometimes losing, huge sums of money in a variety of speculative arenas, from a couple hundred bucks at poker tables, to millions shorting oil futures around the US invasion of Kuwait, to making start-up investments in companies that were ultimately worth billions. The book does all of this in simple language that all aspiring speculators can understand.

To anyone starting down the path of speculation with limited funds as I did, I recommend venturing first into the public stock market. In my case, each time I achieved what I term a "Leppo Surge" (my total liquid net worth multiplied severalfold over a twelve- to eighteen-month period), I focused on the stock market. On the other hand, readers who have already amassed some capital may find my tactics for start-up venture capital of particular interest.

And while I confirm some of the tenets of trading – the trend is your friend, don't listen to stock tips, and don't try to catch a falling knife – I also reveal new insights into reading the market's many "tells." It's one thing to confront a faceless, nameless market. It's quite another to see that market as a living, feeling entity that reacts to world events, that rises and falls based on illusion and widespread belief. And it's still another thing to wrestle with the politics of a start-up, to speculate on the egos and ambitions of the people sitting right in front of you.

A long time ago, I promised myself that whenever I made a mistake in speculation, I would own it. In *The Speculator's Mosaic*, I give the would-be speculator all of it – the good, the bad, and the oh-my-God-why'd-I-do-that. I'm careful to detail not just my successes, but also – or especially – my mistakes and the significant insights I gained from them. With any luck, my insight will save many readers from making the mistakes I made and give them a solid footing for their own adventure in speculation.

While I do claim some unique speculative wrinkles, much of my journey comes from traveling the paths others have trod. As Sir Isaac Newton famously wrote, "If I have seen further it is by standing on the shoulders of giants." And as German philosopher Georg Hegel so aptly observed, "We learn from history that we don't learn from history."

The Speculator's Mosaic is a short book both because I am lazy and because I tried to be succinct. But I did indulge in what at first looks to be a detour due to my love of history. What I'd studied and written about Byzantium weakened my efforts at compactness. As a result, the reader will get a taste of the Empire of Illusion.

I offer my key tactic for how someone as lazy and good at rationalizing as I am could write a book. More than any other single discipline, professional writers will assign fixed chunks of time to sitting down to write. They mostly carve out a fixed portion of the day – usually several hours. I read that one of my favorite writers, Lee Childs, carves out a fixed portion of each year. Regardless of whether it's a fixed portion of a day, week, month, or year, the key is to create a routine. In my case, I started with fifteen minutes of writing after returning from my morning workout. What you hold in your hands right now is the result of my routine.

Robert Leppo

PART I

THE FIRST PIECE OF THE MOSAIC

CHAPTER ONE

Poker and the Advent of Emotion

In early June of 1964, the Cameo Club (located in the heart of what was known as Silicon Valley) was known primarily as a strip joint, but even though I had just turned twenty-one, I was more interested in what went on in the back room. It was poker – lowball draw poker. I had been playing poker in college and had been winning because the competition was mostly clueless. But this was different. It involved grown men. They played better.

One night, I got there at around 8 p.m. ready to play the busiest and most profitable six hours of the week. I sat down. All I needed was some decent cards. But hand after hand my cards were bad, hand after hand. Hour upon hour my frustration and losses grew. By 11 p.m. and much more by midnight, the emotion of anger tempted me to buckle, to start playing mediocre hands. But another emotion intervened: a newfound reservoir of patience. And so I continued to wait, throwing away hand after hand after hand. Then at 1:40 a.m., things turned. In the final twenty minutes, I had four winning hands, and I walked out of the card room at 2 a.m. after winning $100.

Over the next thirteen months – until I graduated in June of 1965 – I won about $1,000 playing after school on Fridays and Saturdays. While I relied on certain visual tactics, like wearing a not-too-new T-shirt and an innocent, bewildered expression, the most important reason I was able to beat the game was that I learned three things: one, to be patient; two, to know what hands to play; and three, to push the good hands hard with big bets.

In order to beat the game, you had to know what hands to play and what to fold. Since I had played other forms of poker – in college, the main game was seven-card hi-lo stud – I found it easy to adapt to this new (to me) game of lowball, where it was the lowest-value hand that won.

In five-card lowball, you are dealt five cards. If I was dealt a hand with no pairs and no card higher than a 9 (the best possible hand would be A2345, called a *wheel*), then I would stand pat and not draw any cards. If the highest card was a 7 or lower, I would have to bet or lose the hand. If I was dealt four cards all 7 or lower and unpaired, I would play and draw one card. All other hands I would throw away.

Many players would play hands that required they draw two cards. Good luck, I thought, rubbing my hands while keeping my bewildered ratty-T-shirt-clad expression on my face.

There was almost no bluffing, and I never bluffed. I didn't need to because the quality of play was low enough that I was able to beat the game.

One player would sometimes draw three cards. This player – TV Bill – held the record for winning the most at a session: several thousand dollars. He also held the record for the biggest losing session, and when, as often happened, he got wiped out, he would then have to go back to repairing television sets (hence his nickname) to get a new stake.

I also got a good lesson in the importance of protocol. One night, I was sitting next to an older man (he must have been all of thirty-five) and we struck up a conversation. After a half an hour, a seat on the opposite end of the same table opened up, and I moved to take it. My next-door neighbor asked if indeed I was going to move, and I said yes. I could tell he was not happy. I came back to play the next day and another player took me aside and said I had insulted the man by moving away from him and "he's a big, strong guy." Fortunately, I had been raised to know what to do. I went over to the man and said, "I understand I was out of line last night, and I owe you an apology."

"I appreciate that," he said. And as he reached out and enfolded my outstretched fingers gently in his massive hand, I knew I had done the right thing.

I should add that in no other poker games I have played in before or after the Cameo Club has changing your seat been a protocol faux pas, but it was at the Cameo Club – at least in the situation I described.

I loved it.

The combination of patience, the knowledge of what cards to play, the discipline to stick to those cards, and my willingness to push a

good hand hard – these all made for a winning strategy with applica-
tion to speculative markets other than poker, although I did not at the
time think of it that way.

Looking back on my early experiences in poker causes me to emphasize the importance of emotion – and as I have developed as a
speculator, I classify emotion as one of the three factors that are tied to
success (i.e., making money) in all forms of speculation. All speculation, including poker, involves winning money from other people who,
for the most part, don't want to lose it but instead are hoping to win.
Which is why I believe the second most important manner in which
emotion pays off for the speculator is figuring out what the actions of
the other players tell you about their emotional state. And what, you
ask, is the *most* important manner in which emotion pays off for the
speculator? It's learning how to maximize your winnings given your
own emotional state.

But during the years when poker was my main as well as first form
of speculation, I always knew that there were other opportunities for a
speculator than poker. But it took years until I began to wonder: Could
my growing power to understand emotion be applied to other – and
larger – markets?

PART II

THE SECOND PIECE OF THE MOSAIC

CHAPTER TWO

The Stock Market – Plunging into the Arena

On January 6, 1975, my office door opened and Bill Griswold came in, a concerned look on his face. "Bob, I'm personally concerned about you. Hey, we both work as security analysts for the same mutual fund. For you to consider buying a stock in the recreational vehicle industry like Coachman means you don't know what's going on in the oil industry. Wage and price controls are causing gas shortages; Saudi Arabia is pushing up oil prices again. Look, Bob, anybody who owns an RV won't know if they might run out of gas driving to the next town. Take my advice as a friend. Stay away."

I managed to keep a somber face and replied, "Thanks, Bill, for thinking of me." But inside, my thoughts were the opposite of somber.

Ha, I thought. I hear the emotion in Bill's voice. I know he's sincere, but I know he's wrong! Because I've visited the company. The stock won't stay cheap once the company reports what I know: that their sales and earnings are starting to rebound.

By understanding the meaning of the emotion in Bill's voice, I took that very day the key step in grasping how a profound understanding of emotion would fuel my success as a speculator.

Coachman was selling that day at five dollars per share, and by not taking Bill's advice but instead putting everything I had (and could borrow) into Coachman, I turned $50,000 into $500K in the next year. And by April Fool's Day of 1977 I was on my own as a private investor.

I was born in Baltimore, Maryland in 1943. When my natural father, Arthur Deute, passed away when I was four, my mother, older brother Bill and I moved to the San Francisco Bay Area. To my great fortune, my mother then married Harrison Leppo in 1949, who adopted both of us. This made for a good comment at the testimonial section of their 40th wedding anniversary party when I got up and said, "Like many of you, I knew my parents before they were married."

Part of my good fortune at growing up with Harrison Leppo as my father was that – apropos of this book – he opened my eyes to speculation. A key manner in which he opened my eyes was by talking about his own investment background, first as a bond salesman in the 1920s, and then during the Great Depression of the 1930s starting an investment management business focused on the American stock market.

Dad had been an investor and money manager for many years and had many stories. His main counsel to me was to be cautious and conservative when investing. But none of the three stories he told me that I remember most vividly were about cautious investing, but rather about three instances when he abandoned his cautious nature.

The first story took place just after the crash of 1929. He had taken severe losses in his personal account and, more important, saw his income as a bond salesman go way down. So he took a major speculative leap. How? He borrowed money from his mother and sold short Westinghouse Electric. The stock continued to decline, and when it had gone down sufficiently to cover his own losses, he covered and paid back his mother.

The second story also happened in the early 1930s. He was still making money by selling bonds and even during the depression had one big buyer of bonds, his main source of business. One day, Dad's partner heard of a major seller back east desperate to sell a block of high-quality municipal bonds at a discount of around $10,000. Dad's partner recommended that they mark up these extra-cheap bonds for their normal markup and make a quick couple of hundred dollars. But Dad disagreed. Instead he marked the bonds up by around $5,000, which still made them cheap, and took them in to show to the buyer. The buyer's eyes widened at the discount, and tapping the bonds, he turned to Dad; "Leppo," he said, "I'll take them."

Dad and his partner both bought new cars the very next day.

The third story took place in the early 1950s. By this time, I was on the scene. Dad had long since switched out of selling bonds and gotten into the investment management business. One day, Dad heard about a private company pioneering in tape recorders called Ampex. He agreed to subscribe to a block of the private stock (we are talking venture capital here), and although he parceled it out mostly to his clients, he did also buy a chunk personally. Ampex thrived and went public. Dad's personal Ampex profits paid for – among other things – a beautiful deck extending out from our Mill Valley, California, living room overlooking Mt. Tamalpais. His Ampex profits also got Dad out of debt for the first time (he paid off the mortgage on the house).

Wow! I thought. That's for me. Little did he know that I had a bent not for cautious conservative diversified investing but rather for speculating wildly in the hope, as Dr. Johnson put it, of achieving "wealth beyond the dreams of avarice." Or, as Andrew Carnegie put it, "Some say don't put all your eggs in one basket, but I say do put all your eggs in one basket and *watch that basket*."

So in the summer of 1956, when I bought my first stock, it was Ampex. I invested $400 and bought twenty shares at $20 per share. One evening I saw my 16-year-old brother Bill coming home from his summer job covered in red dust from stacking bricks all day long at the local brickyard. How much had he made from a heavy day's work? Twenty dollars. I opened the evening paper and learned that Ampex had gone up a full dollar per share, making me $20. Aha! I thought I had found the philosopher's stone.

This set the stage for my focus on the purely speculative. Unlike Dad's taking a position in Ampex as a private company, Ampex as a publicly traded stock neither knew or cared that I owned 20 shares. And I could buy or sell at a moment's notice. Pure speculation.

READING ABOUT SPECULATION: THE NEXT BEST THING TO DOING IT

However, such early trading coups were very infrequent and never amounted to any real money. I did, however, make an important nonfinancial coup.

Sniffing the political and military winds, I joined the California National Guard. Only weeks later, President Johnson escalated in Vietnam, which instantly filled up the National Guard to the max. This delayed my serving six months' basic training, which blocked my getting a job in private industry, so I went to work for the State of California in Sacramento in December of 1965. Now that I had a steady income of $500 per month, I could start speculating in the stock market. I was also armed with an accounting course I had taken in the summer of my junior year of high school.

The First (And Greatest) Book

One day, during my lunch hour, I was browsing at a local bookstore and came across a paperback entitled *Reminiscences of a Stock Operator*. It was an account of how a young, initially penniless teenager (called Larry Livingstone in the book, though based on the legendary speculator Jesse Livingston in reality) made a huge fortune by speculating in the American stock market. The impact of this book on my career as a speculator has been lifelong. Almost all of the other books or articles I had read about the stock market up to that point emphasized the importance of the logical and rational, such as sticking to companies that were at a good value and knowing financial accounting – i.e., corporate income statements and balance sheets – and the importance of reading the footnotes. But *Reminiscences* was different. It told a series of stories about how Larry Livingston learned to beat the market (through often bitter experience, because many of the vignettes involved losing money or missing the boat) and how the tactics the speculator in the book used often had little to do with logic or value but instead emphasized emotion.

Two Vignettes from Reminiscences of a Stock Operator

Sleeping Point.

When a millionaire is right, his money is merely one of his several servants. Losing money is the least of my troubles. A loss never bothers me after I take it. I forget it overnight. But being wrong – not taking the loss – that is what does the damage to the pocketbook and to the soul.

> You remember the Dickson G. Watts story about the man who was so nervous that a friend asked him what was the matter.
> "I can't sleep," answered the nervous one.
> "Why not?" asked the friend.
> "I am carrying so much cotton that I can't sleep thinking about it. It is wearing me out. What can I do?"
> "Sell down to the sleeping point," answered the friend.

It's a Bull Market.

Here's another illuminating story.

Elmer Harwood rushed into the office, wrote out an order, and gave it to the clerk. Then he rushed over to Mr. Partridge. His name was Partridge, but they nicknamed him Turkey behind his back. Well, Elmer told Turkey, "Mr. Partridge, I have just sold my Climax Motors. My people say the market is entitled to a reaction and that I'll buy it back cheaper. So you'd better do likewise. That is if you've still got yours.

"Yes, Mr. Harwood, I still have it, of course!" said Turkey gratefully. It was nice of Elmer to think of the old chap.

"Well, now is the time to take your profit and get in again on the next dip," said Elmer... "I have just sold every share I owned."

But Mr. Partridge shook his head regretfully and whined, "No! No! I can't do that!"

"What?" yelled Elmer.

"I simply can't!" said Mr. Partridge. He was in great trouble.

"Didn't I give you the tip to buy it?"

"You did, Mr. Harwood, and I am very grateful to you. Indeed I am, sir. But –"

"Hold on! Let me talk! And didn't that stock go up seven points in ten days? Didn't it?"

"It did, and I am much obliged to you, my dear boy. But I couldn't think of selling that stock."

"You couldn't?" asked Elmer, beginning to look doubtful himself. It is a habit with most tip givers to be tip takers.

"No, I couldn't."

"Why not?" And Elmer drew nearer.

"Why, this is a bull market!" The old fellow said it as though he had given a long and detailed explanation.

Want to know more? I thought so; read the book. But I will say this last vignette does the best job of reinforcing why it is so important as a speculator to know where you are in the cycle.

Another major difference between *Reminiscences* and the other books on the stock market I had read was concentration. When Livingston found a stock he liked, he would often put his entire net worth in that one stock and borrow heavily (i.e., go on margin) from his brokers to boot. He would protect himself by being always ready to sell out at a small loss if the price turned against him. And he would not care whether the stock was historically high but rather how strong the momentum was building. And just as influential on me was the episode he recounted about going bankrupt through losing speculation, and how he then made back what he had lost.

Wow! This was what I wanted to do, I thought.

Four Other Authors Who Have Aged Well

In the 1960s, I read a number of books on speculation by various authors, but there are four authors I found the most helpful.

Phil Fischer describes his success as a pioneer of the growth stock strategy of investing in his book, *Common Stocks and Uncommon Profit*. Benjamin Graham focuses on finding cheap stocks and pays little attention to the growth outlook in two books, *The Intelligent Investor* and, for those who want to learn how an in-depth knowledge of accounting can discover which stocks are truly cheap, *Security Analysis*. Third is the famous speculator and advisor to presidents, Bernard Baruch's *My Own Story*. And, fourth, *How I Made $2M in the Stock Market* by Nicholas Darvas, who details how he used the price action of individual stocks (termed *technical analysis*) for maximum profitability.

So, at this stage in my budding speculative career, I had learned about multiple strategies for speculation but had made no progress on trying to figure out what strategy would work best for yours truly.

HARVARD BUSINESS SCHOOL, MINUS 90 PERCENT

While at college and at my peak in multiple-choice-test savviness, I took the test for business school and got a good score. In early 1967, I was called into the army for basic training, which ended in time for me to enter Harvard Business School that September.

While I learned many things at Harvard Business School, how to speculate successfully was not one of them. I had saved up about $5,000 when I arrived at Cambridge. And when I graduated in June of 1969, I had about $500. Why had I lost 90 percent? In October of 1967 shortly after arrival, I heard a couple section mates talking about a stock they liked – Acme Missile and Construction – that had been moving up in price and had, they thought, a bright future. So I took almost all my money and bought six-month and ten-day calls on the stock above the market. Unfortunately, after I bought the calls, the stock went down and my calls (bought for 90% of my money) expired worthless. In my own mind, I changed the name of Acme Missile and construction to "Pimple Products." I had not yet learned to stay away from tips (one of the lessons from the book that I remembered but continued to ignore). When I heard something that sounded good, the emotion of greed took over. We'll get back to that word *emotion* later.

Two More Favorite Books

While I always put *Reminiscences* as number one among the most important books anyone considering speculation should read, in 1967, while I was at HBS, the second-best book was published: *The Money Game* by Adam Smith (no, not the original *Wealth of Nations* Adam Smith, but a 1960s money manager turned essayist named George Goodman using "Adam Smith" as a pseudonym). His essays on the two-time rise and fall of Harry, on how poor Grenville played catch-up, and on lunch at Scarsdale Flats are engraved forever in my mind. And in his sequel, *Supermoney*, he introduced his readers to a then unknown money manager in a conversation with Benjamin Graham, who proposed that Goodman, a.k.a. Adam Smith, work on a new edition of one of Graham's books.

"There are really only two people I would want to work on this," Graham said. "You're one and the other is Warren Buffet."

"Who's Warren Buffett?" Goodman asked.

What *The Money Game* did for me as a speculator was to reinforce the power of emotion in determining the success or failure of a speculator. One ignored emotion in favor of rationality at one's peril. Or, put another way, those who think there is a difference between investments made on the basis of prudence and rational calculation and investments made on the basis of hope and greed are wrong. It's all speculation.

Another theme that *The Money Game* reinforced was the power of cycles in speculation. Nothing goes up (or down) forever. Things go in cycles. What things, you ask? All fads having to do with speculation. At the time (we are talking of primarily of the late 60s), technical analysis was in favor, as were conglomerates, as were the go-go funds and Gerry Tsai, as were the Senior Sisters of Growth (IBM, Xerox, and Polaroid). But remember, says Adam Smith, for those who forget that cycles change, the winds blow cold.

Adam Smith's book *The Money Game* has had an impact on my speculative career second only to that of *Reminiscences of a Stock Operator*. One key to this impact is learning the importance of cycles. This concept was later reinforced by my third-favorite book, *The Alchemy of Finance* by George Soros. From my collegiate minor in economics, I had grown comfortable – even complacent – with the idea that if prices in markets got too high or too low, they would inevitably revert back to the mean under the pressure of equilibrium. So when I first read *The Alchemy of Finance*, I resisted Soros's counter insight that in certain markets, such as currency markets or public stocks in new industries, prices could go to great extremes for considerable periods of time because many of the people observing the price changes were speculators who, by their buying or selling, affected the prices they were observing. Fortunately, I reread the book and learned not only that Soros's insight was true; just as important, I learned that I too was vulnerable to having fixed ideas, such as the power of equilibrium, that were not always true.

CHAPTER THREE

Oh, It's Capital

In the spring of 1969, I experienced something close to the courtship ritual that many debutantes go through as companies wanted to hire us soon-to-be-newly-minted Harvard Business School graduates, and I was in the top third of the class academically (barely, I think). I got six job offers in my chosen area of Wall Street. Many of the losers, who will remain nameless, though appreciated, ultimately went under, but not the winner – Capital Research, led by Jon Lovelace (now known as the Capital Group and the manager of the American Funds Group). I was already, at twenty-five, savvy enough to take the Capital offer, even though it paid the least ($1,100 per month, if memory serves). I arrived in the LA offices of Capital Research in June of 1969 and was soon designated the transportation analyst (airlines, railroads, trucking, shipping). I started saving over thirty percent of my salary and for the next two years stuck to a pattern of personal speculation. I would save $2–3,000 and put it into some stock that seemed good to me, often on margin, as I wanted to get rich fast. The result: my personal portfolio went nowhere and sometimes vanished, once again. One reason was that I was focused on my job and therefore spent most of the time on the transportation industries I had been assigned.

Of course, being new to LA, I met friends my age who were involved in the stock market. The two most important (outside the company) were Bob Duggan and Reece Duca, who at the time were partners. I had moved to an apartment right on the beach (well, on the rocks) just south of Topanga Canyon, and by chance the tenant moving out was Trish Duggan. When I told her that I was in the investment business, she said, "Well, you should meet my husband and his partner—they're in the stock market too."

And so I did. The two of them had an investment strategy based heavily on researching upcoming IPOs and being able to get good positions in the IPOs they chose, in part by using "hungry bank" financing – a tactic they had learned from a UC Santa Barbara professor named Herb Kay. More recently they had used in-depth research to find publicly traded growth stocks they felt had promise. When I met them, they were focused like a laser on Ponderosa Systems, a steak restaurant food chain. The company was in financial straits, with a leveraged balance sheet. The company was, however, still opening new restaurants. Reece and Duggan went and visited every store opening, met the store manager, and got info on how each opening was going. And the openings were doing very well. Most new units were generating positive cash flow from the beginning. Meanwhile, one of the Ponderosa directors was so concerned about the leveraged balance sheet that he sold Reece and Duggan a major block of his stock.

After the sale closed, the director said, "You know, Ponderosa Systems is going under."

And they replied, "No, it's not." And the stock went up tenfold over the next two years.

As impressed as I was by Reece and Duggan's success, I was adamant in my own mind to stay away from buying stocks they recommended rather than ones I had researched and come up with myself. (By this time, the experience with Acme Missile was seared into my speculative brain.)

As young speculators in LA, Duggan and Reece invited me to brainstorming sessions on the investment outlook. I remember pontificating at one at a local restaurant until interrupted by their old professor, Herb Kay. "Leppo, I'd pay more attention to you if you were successful. Get rich and then we'll pay more attention. Get rich, Leppo."

That shut me up (temporarily).

CYCLES AND FADS: AIRLINES AND CB RADIO

As a newly minted airline analyst, in late 1969 I had to focus on the airline industry. While air traffic was growing rapidly in the 1950s, airline stock prices were not favored because the federal government's regulatory body, the Civil Aeronautics Board, or CAB, would hold down the prices the airlines were allowed to charge. But in the early

1960s, the airlines were converting from piston engines to jet engines. This new technology was so efficient that overall costs actually declined for several years, even while the jet's faster speed made airline traffic much more appealing to consumers. As a result, traffic grew faster than the airplane manufacturers, such as Boeing, could keep up with demand. So as a surge in earnings began, the industry gained a reputation as a growth industry. However, this transition was largely complete and earnings were well in decline by the time I arrived at Capital.

Once the stock market bottomed in June of 1970, airline stocks began to rebound, propelled by the memories of how strongly earnings had surged in the recent past. But since the CAB was back at its normal stand-off by holding down prices and reducing the profit outlook, the period of considering airlines as growth stocks was shown to be a one-time fad. I was, fortunately, smart enough to recognize that the airlines' booming earnings and stock market rise of the mid-1960s was indeed a one-time phenomenon, and I was able to dissuade Capital from loading up on airline stocks in the early 1970s.

You would think that, having analyzed correctly that the growth potential of airlines would not rebound, I would avoid fads in the future. But as you will read later, I loaded up on a CB radio stock – Dynascan – in 1977, hoping strongly that the industry would rebound. But the evidence was there that it never would. I just didn't see it.

A KEY REVELATION

Finally, at the beginning of 1972, I had a revelation. Perhaps the reason I was getting nowhere with my personal speculation was that I had no strategy. Surely, I could do better than falling for the latest tip.

So for the first time, at age twenty-eight, I arrived at a personalized investment/speculative strategy – one based on my own strengths and assets.

Here is this first strategy. Because I worked at a major financial institution, I had access to its investment library, which contained shelves of expensive publications unavailable to the typical freelance speculator. Specifically, Capital subscribed to the *S&P Daily News*. Every day, S&P sent out a newsletter consisting of all the earnings reports that publicly traded stocks had just released. The first step in my newly minted strategy was to scan the *Daily News* each day and look for companies whose quarterly revenues had grown at least 30 percent from the previous year and whose stocks were moving up. Then, on an adjacent shelf, I took down the S&P loose-leaf volume that had more comprehensive info on all publicly traded companies, and based on that, I tried to determine if I thought the company's stock price would continue to grow. What came out of this was a laser company called Spectra Physics, which was growing quickly by providing lasers used largely in the construction industry for accurate measurements. And the stock was hitting new all-time highs…

Aha, I thought. A growth stock with more to come! This strategy was heavily based on what Jesse Livermore had detailed in *Reminiscences*.

I should mention that at Capital Research, before you could buy a stock, you first had to present the idea to the investment group so that any portfolio manager who wished to could buy the stock in one of our funds before any employee (like me) could buy it personally. But not one of the portfolio managers wanted to buy the stock (in large part because – hey, I was a transportation analyst, and what did I know about high-tech deals like lasers?). I put all I had into the stock and went on margin to the max to boot. The stock continued to rise dramatically during 1972 and I bought more (and went on more margin) as it rose. Then I found a second stock, Action Industries, which was a specialty retailer and it, too, surged obediently. By December of 1972, I had turned $10,000 into $100,000 (before taxes, of course, but you could get both a capital gains treatment and also delay paying any taxes until well into 1973).

As 1973 started, my thought was that I had compounded my net worth tenfold in one year. All I had to do was repeat that in 1973 and I would be a millionaire by the age of thirty! Life was good. I bought a new Datsun 240Z (at the recommendation of one of my bosses, the portfolio manager and amateur race car driver Bob Kirby) and two suits (from Duggan's tailor Frank Hoffer, which Bob Kirby, harkening to my Spectra Physics win, dubbed my "laser suits"), and I continued the hunt for the next big winner. I referred to this sparkling success as a Leppo Surge, which I defined as a severalfold increase in my liquid assets over a twelve- to eighteen-month span.

Emotionally (and you will read more about this), I felt I had made a giant leap away from speculating randomly. Having access to a major financial library, including the *S&P Daily News*, gave me just the edge I needed to assure successful speculation. What could possibly go wrong?

CHAPTER FOUR

The Bear Market Intervenes

What went wrong was 1973 and the start of a vicious bear market. I had been warned by Jon Lovelace's focus on the presidential cycle and the fact that the first year after a presidential election was typically weak for the market. This was particularly true because the White House denizen (Nixon) had been playing a game of pumping the economy up while constraining inflation (i.e., the 1971 imposition of wage and price controls combined with breaking the last connection between the value of the dollar and the price of gold), and Nixon, now safely reelected, was letting the piper be paid in the form of a recession and a severe market crash.

As the stock market started its long decline in 1973, my dream of being a millionaire at thirty was one of the victims. As my net worth started to decline – $100,000, $90,000, $80,000 – I experienced for several months the well-known feeling of the deer caught in the headlights. But because I was on margin and owed significant money with the stocks as collateral, I remembered Dr. Johnson's famous insight into human nature – "the prospect of being hung on the morrow wonderfully concentrates the mind" – and bailed out with about $60,000 left. How humiliating.

POETIC INTERLUDE

Here are some lines from *If* by Rudyard Kipling:

> *If you can make one heap of all your winnings*
> *And risk it on one turn of pitch-and-toss,*

And lose, and start again at your beginnings,
And never breathe a word about your loss…

To find out which portion of the poem I did *not* subscribe to, read on.

TRYING ANOTHER STRATEGY

As 1973 wore on, I looked for new stocks using my now-veteran strategy of high growth. Alas, I didn't find many, in part because the economy was in a nasty recession, which reduced the ability of any company to grow dramatically.

Clearly, a new strategy was needed. And I found one. This time I looked for value, not growth. I looked for companies that were selling at a low – really low – price to earnings.

And so I invested all my remaining funds in Nuclear Dynamics, which despite its name was a coal company selling at two times earnings. At the time, energy prices were up. The oil-producing cartel – OPEC – had responded to Nixon's wage and price control policy with massive price increases, which flowed into other fuels, including coal.

THE BEAR MARKET CRUMBLES MY RECORD AT MY FIRM

I should shift from my personal speculative history to the related subject of my checkered investment research career at Capital Research. At Capital, each analyst also managed a portfolio focused on the stocks he or she was responsible for. In the first three years of my experience with Capital, my portfolio results were well ahead of the averages. Note that most of this period coincided with a bull market that began in early 1970 and ran through December of 1972. On top of this, I had had a great personal speculative year in 1972. As a result, my success with Spectra Physics thus amplified an arrogance that spread over to my responsibilities with Capital. But then 1973 commenced, and down went not only the overall market but also the stocks I was recommending (and owned) in my company portfolio. How the bear market dealt with my arrogance can best be seen in how I dealt with two stocks that I had recommended the company buy: SeaTrain and Leaseway.

SeaTrain was in the container-shipping industry, and playing second fiddle to mighty SeaLand. It was not only smaller but also financially more leveraged. The SeaTrain stock had dropped about 50 percent to $15, so I thought it had to be getting cheap. So, along with Bob Kirby, I went to see them in New Jersey. The two principals shared adjoining desks, which caused Mr. Kirby to compare them to then-popular performing pianists who shared adjoining pianos, Ferrante and Teicher. And so I recommended Capital buy it, and we did. In the following year, the stock went down and down, but I hung in there (well, actually, it was the shareholders of the Capital Research funds who were hanging in there). It was agonizing to watch as week after week, month after month, the stock declined. Ultimately we sold out for less than $1 per share. The emotional cost of being responsible for such a steady loser bled me of the ability to focus on other issues.

Leaseway was at first just the opposite. It was a big truck-leasing company with major customers such as GM and then-mighty Sears Roebuck. I recommended it to Capital near the bottom of the vicious 1970 bear market, and it moved up dramatically. By the end of 1972 I was getting nervous and recommended that we sell. We sold a tiny fraction, but once the bear market began, down went Leaseway. Once again I felt the agonizing feeling of watching one of the stocks I had recommended go down precipitously.

What I learned from the SeaTrain experience was to focus more on the better companies in an industry rather than (as in the case of SeaTrain) a cheaper stock that was a more leveraged also-ran.

My best friend and indeed key mentor Don Smith went for stocks largely on the basis of their cheapness (particularly low price-to-book stocks), but that left me feeling dissatisfied, or rather incomplete. Yes, I liked the idea of focusing on cheap stocks based on price to book. But how could I incorporate the lessons of Phil Fischer?

CHAPTER FIVE
Greed Is (Can Be) Profitable

Understanding how I use the emotion of greed in speculation is critical to my technique. How? It's tied to another emotion that I have in large measure: laziness. If I followed the advice of the typical financial planner and diversified into a large number of positions, then because I am lazy and good at rationalization, I would not remain on top of the various positions.

But by contrast, when I am heavily involved in a stock, my greed gets involved, including constantly contemplating how much I can lose if I am lax in watching the position (stock price) deteriorate. It is true that I often – particularly on the short side, but also sometimes with new long positions – use stops to limit my losses. But I find for someone with my mindset concentrating my positions – I typically want to have my liquid portfolio in between three and five major/core positions – guarantees that I watch them more closely.

Another part of the "watching" is being aware of my emotional state re: each of the positions. If a day comes when, as I run down how I feel about each of the major positions, I notice (and I have trained myself to be conscious here) I come across one where I have a negative emotion, like fear of loss or nervousness about being unable to address or counter some new research about the stock or industry whose negativity I have difficulty in countering, I don't ignore it. Instead, I burrow in. Typically, I will update my knowledge of the stock (or commodity future, for that matter) with the goal of getting the new information that restores my feeling of confidence about the stock, or if I can't, I either sell or at a minimum put in tight sell stop orders.

From my earliest speculative beginnings (i.e., poker), I have gone

180 degrees opposite from Kipling's advice. Not the part about "make one heap of all your winnings and risk it," I have done that many times; rather, I mean the part about "never breathe a word about your loss." Instead, my pattern after taking a big loss in a speculation is:

Look in the bathroom mirror. Hit myself upside the head while shouting, "How could I be so stupid?" Hit, hit. I figure out what I did wrong and what lesson I can learn from the experience and then openly – and I do mean openly – talk about my latest disaster whenever the subject comes up (and often I'm the one deliberately bringing it up).

This process has paid huge dividends. Most importantly, I need spend no energy worrying about what other people may think or trying to figure out how to conceal my debacle. Also, since everybody hears the same message, I need spend no energy trying to remember what I said about it to whom.

Being an independent speculator with just my own money on the line helps in continuing this process. Having no fiduciary responsibility to anyone else for the money lost is liberating. It allows me to exercise what I think is one of my greatest strengths in speculation: I put losses behind me with dramatic speed and with the minimum of emotional scars, so that I don't miss any new opportunity because I'm either plagued with guilt or obsessing over Whittier's famous lines: "Of all sad words of tongue or pen, the saddest are these, 'It might have been.'"

The one time I veered from independent speculation in a major way was in 1990, starting and running a commodity futures fund to earn a salary. When in the fund's second year, I made several losing trades. I felt paralyzed by guilt and shut down the fund. Brrrrr! Never again.

THE EMERGENCE OF EMOTION

By the end of 1974 my arrogance had crumbled, along with both my personal portfolio, which had dropped from $100,000 to $50,000, and my portfolio at Capital, filled with SeaTrain and Leaseway.

In this crisis, I pondered a change in my investment philosophy and came up with a revelation.

I felt I had to find a strategy for speculating in the stock market that would have two attributes. First, it had to work; and second (and just as important), it had to fit my personality. For the first time, I specifically included my emotions in analyzing how I would invest.

The strategy I came up with for personal speculation started with the fact that since I had so little money I could look at the whole range of at least five thousand publicly owned stocks. I knew I could not analyze five thousand stocks. I could not analyze five hundred stocks. But maybe I could analyze fifty stocks. The size of this number fit with how I had screened stocks in my previous strategy, by skimming the S&P Daily News. But clearly I needed a way to go from five thousand possibilities to fifty – to cut my universe by 99 percent. I called this "the initial screen." Note that my previous initial screen had not been industry specific but instead consisted only of those companies that by chance were the ones reporting earnings on the latest edition of the S&P Daily News.

But why could not my initial screen be industry specific? I had the huge benefit that in my job I was reading the financial press (*Wall Street Journal, Barron's, Forbes*, etc.). I decided to screen while reading articles in the financial press. This meant the new screen would have to be less quantitative and more qualitative. Specifically, I started looking for articles concerning specific industries that were filled with gloom. The articles I was looking for were ones with a headline saying something like, "such and such an industry is going into a state of" – wait for it – "*collapse.*" This meant that unlike many speculators who focus on stocks in industries in which they have prior work or academic experience (like computer programmers focusing on the software industry, or MDs focusing on health care), my strategy was specifically *not* industry specific but instead would be collapse specific.

I should mention here that I was emotionally primed for such a contrarian strategy. *The Reminiscences* had examples of this, as did Humphrey Neill in his book *The Art of Contrary Thinking*, as well as my reading in military history.

One industry that I had research responsibility for was recreation, although I had not done much there. I did recommend and buy Coleman (the Coleman Lantern camping company), and I was aware the recreation industry in general was hurt by the recession. In late 1974, one of the industries in recreation that had been most hammered was recreation vehicles or RVs, including travel trailers like Airstream and motor homes like Winnebago. The more I thought about it, the more appealing investing in the RV industry became. The wage and price controls had led to actual shortages of gasoline, meaning that a consumer for the first time could no longer be sure they could fill up their car or truck or – yes – RV. And sales of RVs had collapsed because of more than just the recession we were in. I could imagine a grandfather announcing to his wife that he wanted to buy an RV so they could take their grandkids to see the great USA only to have her point out that he was crazy if he thought he could take her beloved grandchildren out of Keokuk only to run out of gas before they got to Dubuque!

So I went to the Capital Research Library and looked at all the publicly traded names of RV companies and found three or four that were doing better financially than the rest. Note that doing well in this lousy environment meant not so much earning the most profits, or even earning profits at all, but rather losing less. I also checked to see if any of the insiders (officers, directors, large shareholders) were buying the stock in the public market.

And so I found myself in December of 1974 traveling down a northern Indiana road (great pie in the Amish-run local diner, by the way) to the headquarters of Coachman.

I met with the CEO and started the conversation by complimenting him on how well the company was doing in what I was sure had to be a tough environment for his industry. My tactic was based on the fact that most of the calls Coachman got from investors would be calls expressing anger at how much the stock price had gone down. I wanted to separate myself in Coachman's mind from those investors and get the CEO off the defensive. It worked too.

Why did Coachman best fit my new strategy? The company was totally focused on the travel trailer portion of the RV industry. The stock had collapsed from $20 to $3 but in the last three months had rebounded from $3 to $5. But even at $5 the stock was selling at a discount relative to its book value. The most recent quarter showed an uptick in sales and a sharp reduction in the loss to the point where it was back in positive cash-flow territory, taking depreciation into account. I asked the CEO about business and he said, "For the first time since wage and price controls went on in 1971, we are able to raise our prices faster than our costs are going up." Another major plus was that a number of the insiders, including top officers of the company, were buying the stock. But perhaps the greatest plus in my mind was that Coachman so believed in the future of the travel trailer industry that it was going all in by acquiring another travel trailer brand. Specifically, Coachman had just acquired Shasta travel trailers from a large conglomerate, WR Grace.

WR Grace had run Shasta into the ground. Was Coachman making any progress in turning things around? The CEO smiled. "Once we bought it, I went out to the Shasta plant, got the Shasta team together, and asked them, 'How can we help you?'"

The Shasta managers said, "Well, as you know, we used to put little wings on the top of both sides of the back of our trailers. It identified the trailer as a Shasta trailer. But when WR Grace took us over, they sent some young business school types who said, 'Those wings have to go. They don't reflect well on the quality image of WR Grace.'"

"So," pursued the Coachman CEO, "how can we help?"

"Could ... could we have our wings back?"

"Absolutely! From now on Shasta has its wings back."

Shasta sales soared!

Out of this conversation, I was reinforced in my belief that as a lone speculator I could make money over time, given the right strategy. And one of the reasons was that big conglomerates like WR Grace provided opportunities for smaller companies like Coachman to benefit from WR Grace's mistakes.

The next step in the story was back at Capital. In order for me to personally buy any Coachman stock, I had to first recommend the stock to everyone in the company. This I did at what was called a "green-sheet meeting," since all such recommendations were printed on a sheet of green paper. It was only because none of Capital's fund managers wanted to place Coachman in any of the funds (largely because the market capitalization of the company was so small at the time) that I was informed that I could buy the stock in my personal account.

Later that same day, into my office came the oil analyst Bill Griswold. He shut the door and said he was greatly concerned that I might be buying an RV stock, because the situation in the oil industry – a combination of gasoline lines caused by wage and price controls, plus the rapid increase in oil prices triggered by OPEC – was so dire for such companies that Bill was convinced I was making a big mistake putting money into Coachman, and he wanted as a friend to talk me out of it.

My reaction while I listened to Bill I will never forget. While I was deferential and appreciative, inside I was rubbing my greedy speculative hands in glee. Here I thought was a very intelligent friend making heartfelt comments, ignorant of the real turnaround already underway at Coachman. I didn't argue with Bill. Instead, the conversation sharply reinforced my confidence that I was in a good speculation.

I then put all my assets ($50,000) into Coachman, ultimately buying over 20,000 shares at an average price of seven (and going on margin to buy much of the stock). A year later, Coachman had climbed to over twenty-five dollars per share. My net worth had been boosted tenfold to $500,000.

Out of this experience, I have been keenly conscious of the importance of considering emotion in the making of speculative decisions. Ever since, I have put focus on what I consider the first key to how I successfully speculate: *emotion*.

HOW I USE EMOTION IN STOCK MARKET SPECU-LATION: THE IMPORTANCE OF MEMES

A political story: In 1969, when Senator Edward Kennedy was embroiled in the Chappaquiddick scandal, I was reinforced in my conviction that Teddy and his liberal beliefs I should oppose. Two years later the Watergate scandal broke. Once Teddy Kennedy announced that he opposed President Nixon because he alleged Nixon was involved in Watergate, I instinctively (yes, emotionally) felt Nixon should be supported. In short I was influenced by the notion that "the enemy of my enemy is my friend."

In the summer of 1974, as I was listening to my car radio, Nixon, who could no longer block key evidence from coming to light, revealed that he had lied about Watergate to the American people. Although I was alone, I remember muttering aloud, "You son of a bitch!" I felt personally betrayed by Nixon's false claims that he did not know about the Watergate break-in. Out of this experience, I quickly concluded that I had been deluded not so much by Nixon's lies, but rather by how entrenched my emotions of disdain for Kennedy and resulting *emotional* support for Kennedy's enemy, Nixon, had become.

I was ripe, therefore, to learning about the theory of memes.

> **Meme** (mēm) *n.* A unit of cultural information, such as a cultural practice or idea, that is transmitted verbally or by repeated action from one mind to another.

The core idea that struck me was to think of a meme as an idea or belief that has attributes of a living organism. Specifically, the belief tries to survive and has defense mechanisms to help it survive. When the belief is challenged, say in a discussion with another person that brings up factual info that counters the belief, the defense mechanism is to recall past experiences that first triggered the belief. Inevitably these experiences have a strong emotional component to them. Once the emotion comes to the fore, the ability to rationally examine the belief on an ongoing basis during the discussion and consider changing it is sharply diminished. This process, I thought, was how a meme defended itself (at least in my own mind).

So, for example, I had a meme that Nixon was telling the truth when he said he knew nothing about the 1972 Watergate break-in before it happened. In my case when that meme was challenged, the meme in my mind, like a living organism, defended itself by bringing up how I felt antagonism toward Nixon's political enemy Teddy Kennedy, because of his conduct at Chappaquiddick. The effectiveness of this defense was largely due to the emotional connection. That emotional connection blocked my rational mind from analyzing the evidence (clearly growing, thanks to the journalists Woodward and Bernstein *et al.*) calmly. That my emotions were involved explains why when Nixon finally confessed to his earlier knowledge in 1974, I reacted with an emotional sense of personal betrayal.

As I thought about this experience, I concluded that the key to a meme's power was precisely to have those emotional defenses at the ready to surge up from my subconscious to block a rational review by my conscious mind of whether the meme was true or false.

One could even say that I had now developed a new meme/belief, which was that when I noticed that I have an emotional reaction – particularly a negative emotional reaction – to some conversation with some person, I needed to switch my attention away from whatever the ostensible topic of the conversation was and focus instead on what was going on emotionally (either in myself or what I could sense from the other person). The emotional side became the dominant factor in the interchange. Or to put it another way, I should forget about the topic and figure out what was behind the upwelling of emotion.

Applying this to speculation, when I analyze an article in which the writer's opinion seems to be based on emotion, I assume that the conclusions in the article are based on selecting those facts that support the writer's emotional stance. And when the writer's emotions agree with my own, I assume I am less likely to learn much.

A final factor revealing why I was open to learning about memes happened during high school.

For the first time in my life, I cheated. The English teacher, Mr.

MacDougall, gave us a quiz during class and then told us the answers for us to self-grade. Never having self-graded anything, I found myself rationalizing why a couple of the mistakes I made were inadvertent and I could change them. Mr. MacDougall caught it and announced that someone had cheated, but he didn't say who. I suffered through the longest three days of my life until finally going to his home to confess.

I have never cheated again nor attempted any cover-up. To this day, whenever the subject of cheating comes up, out of my subconscious wells the meme that I would never cheat fueled by the emotion of those despairing three days.

Consider the political axiom: "It's not the crime, it's the cover-up."

The experience also turned me away from covering up any of my own mistakes, even honest mistakes. As a result, whenever I make a speculative mistake of any kind, I immediately acknowledge it. This avoids a replay of the truly existential despair and concealment of those three days trying to cover up my cheating – brrrr!!!

Remember the lines of Kipling in the previous chapter: "If you can make a heap of all your winnings and risk it on one turn of pitch-and-toss; and lose, and start again at your beginnings; and never breathe a word about your loss." I say, "Not this cowboy." When I lose money, I go to the other extreme. I admit it openly. I even bring it up. The relief of not being embarrassed by trying to conceal an important mistake is a *huge* benefit.

CHAPTER SIX
Summarizing My Stock Market Strategy

Ever since the Coachman triumph, I have focused my stock market speculation on this strategy: I begin by constantly scanning for industries that are entering a state of collapse; next, I determine whether the collapse is permanent (for example, was the industry a fad, or to put it another way, was the industry's growth phase based on factors that had peaked and were unlikely to recur?), or in contrast whether the downturn is cyclical and tied to factors that given time are likely to rebound.

If I conclude the odds are good that the industry will rebound, then I screen all the stocks involved in the industry and pick the two or three that on the earnings numbers are the best of the worst. If the industry collapse is so precipitous that all the participants are losing money, then the best would be the one that has financial staying power: that is, the one that is losing the least and has the strongest financial position in terms of the least debt and the most cash.

I seldom buy any stock selling at more than two times its book value and give extra points to those selling near – or even better, at a discount – to book value. When analyzing the top candidates, I give extra points to those where there is insider buying and those that are getting deeper into the collapsing industry by acquiring other brands then available at bargain prices. I then have conversations either by phone or by traveling to the company's headquarters. I try to differentiate myself from other investors by complimenting management on how well, compared to their competition, they are navigating through the tough times.

I learned from my mentor Don Smith in 1970 to create a table to compare stocks I was considering investing in. My table has the name of the stock, current EPS, expected EPS in eighteen months, expected PE in eighteen months, current price, and price in eighteen months; this yields in the column at the far right of the table the percentage gain. As new information comes in, I update my table. I prune the portfolio by selling the stocks that have the least potential, because I cut my estimate of eighteen-month-out earnings, or because a stock has moved up and gotten ahead of itself, or finally because I need cash to buy a new stock. I use my emotions as a factor in which stocks I buy. I will typically buy one-third to one-fifth of my final position and stop to see what my emotions tell me. If greed fills me about the new stock, I buy more; if fear wells up, I track down the source of the fear. Often there is some wrinkle about the stock that I need more information on, so that I either resolve the fear or reverse course and sell the stock.

This table gives the best answer to the question I am often asked: "Well, if you like stock A at $10 per share, at what price [or when] will you sell?" To which I answer, "I typically sell only when a new stock has significantly higher potential than one of my existing investments."

I should add that this table provides a discipline that reduces – though, alas, for someone as lazy as me, does not eliminate – the complacency I am prone to when things are going my way. And in recent years this complacency has – alas – extended to not filling out the table at all in long stretches.

Once I garnered enough net worth to live on, I began limited diversification, looking for three to five stocks in at least three different industries.

MR. SMITH AND A FORK IN THE EMOTIONAL ROAD

As 1976 dawned, I was flush with the success of my new strategy. And as I looked for other industries to try it with, I came across the steel industry, which had been hammered during the recent recession and still sported a number of cheap stocks. I talked this over once again with Don Smith. He agreed that the steel industry stocks were underpriced, and he was buying some in the portfolio he managed for the company. Don gave priority to finding the cheapest steel stocks (as measured by price-to-book value), whereas I had moved on to finding the best steel companies, even though they might be far from the cheapest. This made sense for both of us from an emotional standpoint. Don felt most comfortable with stocks so cheap that he felt the downside was limited. I, on the other hand, got most excited (note the different emotional state) buying stocks I felt had the most upside, and I felt the best companies had a better chance of being perceived by institutions as growth stocks.

From a literary standpoint, you could say Don was more Benjamin Graham and I was more Phil Fischer. A related difference between the two of us was that Don was the more cautious, and I was the more bold. This may explain why every stock I bought, regardless of price, I would assure my friends "is going to a hundred dollars per share, and I'm not selling. When you hit a home run you don't stop at first base!" It also may explain why a friend at the time tagged me as *Mad Dog*.

ON MY OWN

In June 1976, within a month of Coachman surging to where I hit my $500,000 net worth target, Capital Research offered me a step up to the position of portfolio manager. I knew I shouldn't take it unless I was prepared to commit to staying with the company for an extended period of time. This presented a dilemma. Should I stay or should I go?

As I thought over how to make the choice, I finally came to the following conclusion: If I woke up at age fifty (which seemed very old at the time), and I was still at Capital, I felt I already knew pretty much what that would be like. Whereas if I went on my own, *I didn't know* what that would be like, and who I would be like at fifty. Which meant that if I stayed at Capital, I would always wonder what it would have been like had I gone out on my own.

On the other hand, if I made the leap I would not have to wonder. And so I leapt. I left Capital Research at age thirty-three on April Fool's Day – April 1, 1977. One factor was personal health. My hearing had started to deteriorate and I wanted the freedom to search out alternative therapies, but the core factor was not wanting to wonder what being on my own would be like.

On April 1, 1977, my final day at Capital, my associates sent me off by singing the "Capital Song" I had written. I moved to San Francisco and opened my new career as a private investor by exiling my suits and ties to the back of the closet. I didn't throw them out, though.

THE NEXT STOCK MARKET EFFORT: A MISTAKEN PRIORITY ON VALUE

In 1977, on my own after moving to San Francisco, I used my stock market strategy. I came up with three industries that fit my criteria: auto insurance, CB radios, and steel.

The auto insurance industry's profit margins were in the dumps, but Progressive Insurance had uncovered and was exploiting a unique niche by focusing on drivers who were higher risk than most and therefore unable to get auto insurance policies at reasonable prices. Progressive had developed cutting-edge methods of analyzing the risks so that they were able to profitably write insurance for wayward drivers that most insurance companies would refuse. But after holding the stock for a few months, I sold out.

My experience in the steel industry was similar. I had read about Nucor in 1975 when it was just starting its rise as a steel producer with small electric furnaces. I went to meet the CEO, Ken Iverson, and he took me on a tour of their local steel mill (tiny by industry standards, turning out a mere 2–300,000 tons of steel per year). Nucor, unlike almost all other American steel producers, was nonunion and paid its employees on a bonus system tied to how productive they were. So, I bought the stock but after a few months sold it for a slight profit.

With Nucor, as was the case with Progressive, I had been in a sense spoiled by Coachman's precipitous rise just after I bought it and missed the spectacular rise both companies achieved in the following years, which in the case of Nucor, Richard Preston chronicled in his *American Steel*.

As I checked out Dynascan, I liked that the industry it was in – CB radios – had collapsed much more than either steel or the auto insurance. Therefore even the financially strongest contender, Dynascan, with its well-known Cobra brand, was selling cheaper (selling at a discount to book value). There were strong reasons that the previous surge in demand for CB radios was a fad that would not rebound, but I failed to give that sufficient weight. Alas, I held on to Dynascan for two years and actually sold at a slight profit, but I had made the huge mistake of focusing on value over growth potential and picking the industry that had declined the most, rather than focusing on industries (both steel and auto insurance) that were much more likely to stay around. Also, the companies I was looking at were small factors in the overall industry, so their better prospects and management had far more room to take market share than the relatively faddish CB radio industry.

PART III

THE THIRD PIECE OF THE
MOSAIC

CHAPTER SEVEN
Where We Are in the Cycle

I have spoken of how my strategy of successful speculation focuses on emotion. The experience with Dynascan highlights the importance of the second key issue for successful speculation: cycles, specifically up-and-down periods of boom and bust that can last for years. Every industry goes through cycles that impact the sales of the participants in the industry. A small change in sales usually triggers a larger change in profits, which in turn (such is the power of investor's emotions) triggers a still larger volatility in stock prices. I planned to feed off this volatility by buying only in industries that were in a state of collapse. But that only worked when the down cycle could be counted on to rebound into an up cycle. But I had walked into investing heavily into one industry whose entire history was one of a single, long, gathering boom that had turned to bust. This meant the odds that demand, which in 1977 was falling, would rebound were far lower than for long-term industries – such as auto insurance or steel.

I didn't lose money in Dynascan because I was right that the company was cheap and would survive the down better than its weaker competitors. But the opportunity cost was significant, because I locked up so much of my cash for two years. A major reason I kept most of my money in Dynascan rather than selling and buying either Nucor or Progressive was because I allowed myself to be locked into the lazy emotion of complacency. Specifically, I had done considerable work identifying and qualifying Dynascan and put a high priority on its being cheaper than the others in terms of price-to-book value. What I was too lazy to do was thoroughly investigate and compare the growth potential of the three stocks. Looking back, it would have been clear to me, even at the time, when I was still learning how to use my strategy, that the growth potential of Dynascan lagged the other two dramatically, both because the prospect for an industry rebound was far higher for either steel or auto insurance than CB radios, and also the market share of both Nucor and Progressive was far smaller in their industries than was the market share of Dynascan, with its leading Cobra brand, in CB radios. I finally saw the writing on the wall in 1979. I had wasted two years.

A related important mistake I made in picking Dynascan was to fail to consider timing when investing in down industries. I was comfortable with the concept of investing in an industry only after the down period had begun. But that begged the question – when did I expect the stocks to hit bottom? I knew the phrase cautioning speculators: *don't try to catch a falling knife*. But I ignored the warning with vigor.

My best cure for this lack is to once again focus on my own emotions. I look for the emotion of desperate greed. When I find it, I buy the stock. When that greed is missing, I know I am better off not buying. I sometimes calibrate by only buying a fraction of a full position and then waiting to see what my emotional state is the following day. If I remain desperately greedy, I buy more. If not, not.

Picking Dynascan over Nucor and Progressive marked the beginning of my recognition that where we are in the cycle of an industry is, along with emotion, one of the major keys to my speculative success. But there was more to learn about cycles, as I was about to find out.

A NEW STOCK MARKET SURGE: CIRCUIT CITY

In 1979, I got intrigued with yet another industry: consumer electronics retailing. This industry was struggling because there was a lack of exciting new products. The boom in color TV that Adam Smith spoke of in *The Money Game* and that the consumer electronics industry had fed off of was over. When I mentioned to a friend, Bill Oberndorf, my interest in consumer electronics retailing, he said, "You should check out Ward's company."

So off I went to Richmond, Virginia, to meet at the headquarters of Wards and see the first of their new retail formats, which was focused on being family friendly, including a daycare center, so parents could drop off their young kids to play while going next door to shop for a TV. I was intrigued, so once again I got into the stock – and then waited. 1979, 1980, 1981…

My mistake here was that once again I was buying prematurely and stubbornly ignoring timing the industry cycle. I should note that one reason the timing on Coachman worked so well in 1975 was that it had already been in the dumps for a couple years before I got into it. Why? Because I only developed my new strategy in 1975 when Coachman's cycle was starting to turn up. Whereas in the case of Wards, the cycle had turned down more recently and not had time to recover. Their new family-friendly larger store innovation was intriguing but too nascent to be noticed by the stock market. But a saving grace in holding on to Wards was that at least it was a participant in a major industry, consumer electronics, that was less vulnerable to being a one-time fad than CB radios had proved to be.

As 1982 dawned, Wards's growth rate had finally begun to surge. Its innovations in consumer electronics store formats were beginning to pay off. The company changed its name to Circuit City and the stock mounted up.

I was considering selling when I mentioned the situation to another friend and savvy investor, John Lee. When I told him that I projected much higher earnings for Circuit City in 1983, he said, "Don't sell now. If you're right on your estimates, the stock has more to go."

I took John's advice and held on for another year, during which time Circuit City stock tripled, and then I did sell out.

DRIFTING

Starting with 1984, the energy and focus I had been devoting to the stock market dwindled. I did not use my strategy to find new industries that were in down cycles. Of course, there were fewer industries going into bad times, as Reagan's supply side tax cuts that became fully effective in 1983 were triggering an overall economic boom. This was best described in Robert Bartley's *The Seven Fat Years*. As the stock market rose, I became increasingly nervous about being heavily invested in stocks, and that became a rationale for becoming complacent and no longer following the rigor of my stock market strategy.

MY STRATEGY ADAPTS: INSIDE MILKEN AND THE INTERNET

The stock market crashed in 1987 and so did my liquid assets. The stock market quickly recovered and then surged even higher. But I concluded the stock market was too high, and I largely stayed out, putting my investment strategy in abeyance.

What I didn't appreciate at the time was that we were all in for a series of dramatic changes in how the stock market worked and therefore how my strategy needed to adapt.

The first change was the criminalizing of inside information. When I was working at Capital, a major part of the job was visiting companies and having interviews with management, which were then detailed in confidential reports inside Capital. Similarly, in 1975 when I went to Indiana and talked to the CEO of Coachman, it was perfectly legal for the two of us to have a private conversation. But in the 1980s, things started to change, and by 1989, with the imprisonment of Michael Milken, everybody knew it. Top management of all publicly traded stocks had been instructed by their lawyers that the emergence of the new insider trading trials meant that having any private conversations about their company's outlook with investors was dangerous and could land violators in the cell next to Mr. Milken.

So, the companies adapted by rigorously restricting talking about the future outlook, particularly the outlook for profits. Instead, public companies increasingly began organizing a single conference call every three months just after the quarterly financial results were announced. This assured that all investors and security analysts got new information on the company at the same time, thus keeping the federal prosecutors at bay. The advantage I got from visiting a company like Coachman or Circuit City was diminishing.

As the 1990s progressed, three other major changes in investing tactics were tied directly to the rise of the Internet.

Financial information websites sprang up. My favorite was Yahoo! Finance, but there were many others such as the Motley Fool and Seeking Alpha. This leveled the playing field in being able to quickly screen for out-of-favor industries and compare within the industries for the best candidates.

Secondly, all companies built their own websites, and if they were publicly owned they would include press releases and all other public financial information.

And finally, for many public stocks, the rise of chat rooms provided another new source of information in deciding what stocks to buy.

IRRATIONAL EXUBERANCE: THE INTERNET TAKES HOLD

Until 1999, I benefitted as a speculator from the rise of the Internet, not by buying publicly traded Internet stocks, but by focusing on the start-up venture market (as I discuss later in this book). But in 1999, with liquid cash high, following Internet-related venture paydays, I thought a number of the Internet stocks were so overpriced that I could make money by shorting them. An excellent book, *Irrational Exuberance* by Robert Shiller, had just come out and added to my conviction that the high prices of a lot of these stocks would soon reverse.

These stocks were based, I thought, on several themes that I thought were illusions; one theme was that a company could be very valuable even though it was losing a lot of money if its Internet traffic was big enough and growing fast enough; a related theme was that an Internet company that was the biggest in a particular sector of the Internet would remain so, and that it would be hard for a newer company to dislodge the incumbent, which had built an entrenched "brand."

Ha! I exclaimed, diving into the short side. As a result, I lost about 10 percent of my liquid assets in around six weeks as those same stocks surged to new highs. I was saved from further folly by my now practiced sensitivity to my emotional state. I woke up at night nervous about the losses. I remembered the advice from John Maynard Keynes, who once said, "The market can remain irrational longer than you can remain solvent."

I quickly covered my shorts.

But having identified shorting Internet stocks as a future opportunity, I continued to watch for the rest of the year 1999, and in the spring of 2000, those same Internet stocks started to flutter from their even more outrageously high prices.

So what did I do? I went back to the short side. And this time it worked. A prominent example will demonstrate why. Exodus Communications was founded in 1994. Exodus secured initial venture funding, got customers for its Internet web hosting service, went public with a market capitalization in the billions, and by the year 2000 was making billion-dollar acquisitions (for stock, to be sure). During this first growth phase, the company never made a profit, but instead fed off the commonly held illusion that spending to become dominant in a niche in the Internet would eventually pay off. Instead, when the Internet bubble peaked in 2000 and prospects declined, it took Exodus only one year to complete the cycle. It declared bankruptcy in 2001.

Other short but similar stories included IVillage and Diba.

I remained focused on the short side of the stock market into 2002, but once the collapse of the overpriced Internet stocks had run its course, I pulled out of the market and stayed out for seven more years – until 2009.

THE SUBPRIME MORTGAGE BUBBLE GETS ME BACK IN THE MARKET

When the Internet bubble burst and the market declined into 2002, it never got cheap enough to tempt me back into using my stock market strategy. The biggest reason it did not get that cheap was because the Bush Administration continued the Clinton Administration tactics of making it progressively easier to buy homes by having the federal government make available (via Fannie Mae financing) mortgages to those increasingly unlikely to be able to service them. The traditional standard was to require a 20 percent down payment to get a mortgage. The extreme of this particular bubble was the issuance of billions of dollars of so-called NINJA mortgages, NINJA describing borrowers possessing:

No
Income
No
Job, no
Assets

While NINJA lasted, it both eased the recession in 2000–2001 and fueled the recovery from 2002 to 2007. *The Big Short* by Michael Lewis, both book and movie, portrays the insanity of this particular bubble in subprime mortgages.

I RENEW THE HUNT: GETTING BACK INTO THE STOCK MARKET

The massive subprime mortgage bubble burst, pushing the stock market in 2008 down to traditional bear market levels by December of 2008. In response, I dusted off my stock market strategy and began actively looking for the next stock to buy. I discovered Huntsman Corporation on December 15, 2008. That was the day Huntsman

Chemical announced that it was to receive $750 million in cash from the private equity firm Apollo. Apollo was one of a group committed publicly to buy Huntsman for $10 billion, and this cash payment got Apollo off the hook. During the previous summer of 2008, arbitrage firms had been propping up the Huntsman stock to only a small discount from the $28-per-share purchase price, speculating that the purchase would likely go through, even though the gathering recession was hurting the profitability of Huntsman's chemical operations. But as the year progressed, Huntsman's stock declined to $5 per share. And then on December 15 the stock crashed further to under $3 per share, thus valuing the entire company with its multibillion-dollar chemical operations at about $700 million. I spent the following weekend analyzing the situation.

I concluded this was a great opportunity because of the emotions within the arbitraging institutions. I thought back to when at Capital Research one of the companies I had recommended reported earnings significantly lower than the company had led me to expect. I was embarrassed big-time. When I was called on the carpet for why I had been wrong, I explained that I had been misled, and since I no longer had confidence in the company, I felt that we should sell the stock, even though it had already gone down.

I thought that a major reason why Huntsman had gone down when announcing it was to receive such a huge cash infusion was because of the emotional reaction of embarrassment/betrayal on the part of the arbitrage owners. On top of which, by selling their position before the end of December, they would not have to report holding any of the stock in their year-end report to their own investors.

Over the ensuing year, Huntsman moved up dramatically and we sold out at $12 per share. While this was in the context of a rebounding market, the more important insight was that my dusted-off stock market strategy was still useful.

CHAPTER EIGHT
What I Look For

The importance of the cyclicality of things can be best illustrated by the story of the ancient king who asked his philosophers for a statement that was always true, and the winner came back with: "This too shall pass."

I focus on three factors in speculation: emotion (I have explored that already), illusion (more on that to follow), and where we are in the cycle (the current subject). I want to review why, of these three major factors, I consider myself weakest in figuring out *where we are in the cycle.*

It all comes back to personality. From an early age I became comfortable with being a contrarian, looking to zig whenever the consensus was zagging. So when I found a contrary investment, whether big triumphs like Coachman or disappointments like Dynascan, I was sucked into investment on the moment rather than more thoroughly reviewing the timing of the industry cycle. This lapse has plagued my investing career. For example, I became very negative in 2004 about the mortgage company Fannie Mae, based on how high the real estate bubble had become. But after being short the stock for several months, I gave up on the short. What was worse, I then ignored the signal of when Fannie Mae stock dropped below $50 per share (despite telling myself how closely I had learned trend following from *Reminiscences of a Stock Operator*). I did not re-short, and therefore I was nothing but an observer as the stock utterly collapsed in 2007–8.

I made an even greater mistake in ignoring cyclicality during the Internet boom/bubble of 1994–2000. My initial venture investments in the Internet generated massive profits as so many Internet start-ups generated cash paydays during the 1997–1999 glory days. But rather than shifting that cash out of Internet investments late in the boom period, I doubled down into new start-up illiquid venture investments. This meant that unlike my speculations in publicly traded stocks (like Dynascan), where I changed my mind on the investment I was locked in with no way to get out.

Oof!!

Yet another important mistake I made re: cyclicality came in 2014 when I started investing in gold mining stocks trying to play the bear market in the price of gold. The scale of this mistake is worth more detailed examination.

THE CYCLE OF MANIPULATION AND ILLUSION

The price of gold and silver surged to new highs in 2012, but then both metals began to decline. As was the case in the 1990s under the Clinton Administration (Treasury Secretary Robert Rubin, a Goldman Sachs alumnus, being a key player), the price of gold was manipulated down. In the 1990s, the manipulation was focused on pushing a number of sovereign states to sell large portions of their national gold reserves. But starting in 2012, the Obama Administration pioneered a new form of manipulation centered on the gold contract on the US futures market: the COMEX.

Every month or two from 2013 through 2015, massive sell orders (and *only* sell orders, *never* buy orders) would be thrown onto the exchange – orders of a thousand contracts or more. Often there would be two or three such huge sell orders thrown at the market in less than one hour. Since each gold contract was for a hundred ounces of gold at an average price of $1,500 per ounce, we are talking about *hundreds of millions of dollars* each time this happened.

I believe these sales were manipulation because any private institution (mutual fund, private equity group, ETF, etc.) needing to sell such quantities of gold, whether physical bullion or, as is the case on the COMEX, paper futures contracts, would never throw such huge orders on the market all at once. Instead the institution would feed the sales out over many days or weeks, primarily to fulfill their fiduciary responsibility to get the best price. But instead, these orders caused an immediate major drop on the price of gold over and over again.

TIMING THE CYCLE AND FOOL'S GOLD (AND SILVER)

In 2012, the price of gold and silver started to roll over, following an enormous twelve-year-long bull market. I not only stayed out of gold and silver but also won a nice bet from someone at the Matrix poker casino that gold would trade over $2,000 per ounce. (This helped offset my losing bets on the presidential election.) But when in early 2013 gold broke dramatically below $1,400, I began to consider going long again.

I had been watching a gold stock, Allied Nevada, and had made small buys when the stock dropped below $40. Because the stock was not cheap (and therefore violated my normal tactic of only taking major positions in beaten-down stocks), I carefully put in a sell stop and got stopped out with a small loss. But when Allied Nevada dropped precipitously to below $10 per share, I got more aggressive. This coincided with further weakness in the price of gold, and I did take a major position at $7 per share. Allied Nevada had emerged as an important producer of gold from their Nevada mine but continued to be squeezed by their heavy debt. I felt that when the price of gold rebounded, Allied Nevada would be a major beneficiary.

Instead, the price of gold did not recover, and I finally sold the Allied Nevada stock at $3. The company ultimately went bankrupt.

I made two major mistakes in the Allied Nevada speculation. In picking the company, I failed to screen all the gold mining stocks and pick from among the best – a key to my previous strategies with stocks like Coachman. But the other major mistake was to once again ignore timing or where we were in the industry cycle. I went into precious metal stocks too early.

What sucked me to precious metal stocks so early in the down cycle?

One key was that I thought back to India in 1982. That year gold, after a huge bull market, had touched $800 per ounce. At those high prices, many Indian citizens (who owned physical gold in the form of Hindu wedding gifts, such as necklaces, bracelets, etc.) came into gold shops and turned in their gold for US dollars. And that turned out to be a good signal for an extended gold bear market that eventually bottomed at $250 per ounce. By contrast, in 2013 there was *no* corresponding rush to the Indian gold shops to sell their bracelets for US dollars. Instead, at $1,300 per ounce, Indian consumers were *buying* gold.

A second reason was China. China in 1981 imported little gold (in large part because the economy was small and individual Chinese were barred by the Communist government from buying gold). But in 2010, buying gold became legal in China, and the amount of gold bought by the much larger Chinese economy surged dramatically.

A third reason was that the mainstream financial media were by and large bearish or neutral on buying gold and silver – in large part because they emphasized that US inflation was low and claimed that gold and silver priced in dollars were unlikely to recover unless US inflation surged, as it had in the 1970s.

A fourth reason that persuaded me to buy was that one of the key factors that pushed prices down in the 1990s and early 2000s was the net selling by governments, mostly in Europe. But this ended in 2007 and I felt it unlikely that it would reemerge as a bearish factor. And that proved to be true.

There was a final reason why I moved most of my liquid assets into one industry. I was uncomfortable putting assets in any other liquid market. The stock market had seen an enormous rise since 2009; the bond market had also risen, due in large part to the government (Federal Reserve) manipulation to suppress interest rates; real estate was by definition not liquid, and I continued avoiding foreign markets (either stocks or bonds).

So it was that armed with all these reasons, when gold dropped below 1400 (down from 1900) and silver dropped below 20 (down from 45), I pounced. How did I pounce? Well, for the most part I pounced by buying not gold or silver but rather gold and silver *mining* companies. They had already dropped, and I was careful (so I thought) to buy only the strongest stocks financially. This of course continued my long-established strategy of looking for industries entering into a state of collapse. The prices of the gold and silver mining stocks I picked had gone down even more than the prices of bullion, meaning they were available at what seemed low prices compared to their assets (book value) – a sign, I thought, that the sellers were emotionally distraught over their losses. Plus, I had a high conviction that an important part of the decline was based on the massive repeated dumping on the COMEX that I felt led to more panicked selling that was counter to what I felt were the bullish fundamentals for gold.

And so, I loaded up on gold and silver mining stocks.

The result was a major drop in my liquid assets as the price of gold continued to decline to under 1100 per ounce by 2015.

What went wrong?

What I had forgotten was how important timing the cycle was. The previous bear market had lasted *eighteen years*, from 1982 to 2000. And here I was thinking a two-year bear market (2011 to 2013) was time enough for a major bottom.

The result was major losses. I had drastically underestimated the length of the gold bear market cycle.

I did save myself from true disaster by holding to my previous dictate of getting *off* margin once my positions started to decline. I remembered the famous warning of my friend Jon Andron: "Double up, triple up, belly up!" And just as important, I cut back ruthlessly on charitable and/or venture capital commitments in the interest of self-preservation. And I maintained my policy of openness, not trying to conceal how much I was losing but, if anything, initiating the mention of it. This may be the greatest single trait that separates me from the typical – or might I say normal – investor. As always, admitting openly my mistakes takes their power or weight away from me. By now the reader should realize how important understanding and working with/using my emotions is to my speculative career.

CHAPTER NINE

Once the Worm Turns

In January 2016, two wonderful things happened. First, gold and silver started to surge. Second, one of our venture deals followed through with a buyout and I got a chunk of cash. This time I put the money mostly into liquid gold and silver mining stocks.

I have always known – and more important always been open in admitting – that I was not the perfect speculator. I have mentioned my personal laziness as being an important flaw. But I do believe the biggest single flaw in my speculative armory has been that I continue to underrate the importance of determining where I am in the cycle – as seen by my 2013 mistake in going long gold and silver prematurely in their down cycle. The mistake was not so much from a percentage of loss basis but rather getting in *too early* – or as it is often described, "trying to catch a falling knife."

That is why the best single tactic for not getting carried out by being wrong on a speculation – whether a stock or a commodity – is to limit my losses going in. Be ready to get out after a small loss.

Notice that the more money you have, the tougher it becomes to stay concentrated for maximum upside (a Leppo Surge). Often the biggest upside is in thinly traded small caps, which by definition are tough to get out of if you change your mind.

CYCLES OF SPECULATIVE INNOVATION

Another important cycle for speculators to understand is the cycle in the profitability of new ways of speculation. This is particularly true in the stock market. Just since the 1960s, we have witnessed the rise and fall of conglomerates (Jimmy Ling), the Go-Go years, the Nifty Fifty, the inflation bubble, the rise of supply-side economics under Reagan and its fall under George H.W. Bush, junk bonds (Michael Milken), the focus on emerging markets, the LBO phase, the subprime mortgage bubble. Even the rise of the Internet suffered a major down cycle in the 2000–2002 market collapse. And there is the recurrent cycle of modes of speculation such as value investing (Graham and Dodd), growth investing, venture capital, and more recently passive investing (index funds, ETFs). And the rise of private equity funds (KKR, et al). And the rise of quants that use computer software algorithms. The list goes on and I predict will never end.

The main lesson of this history is that one can expect that the effectiveness of all new speculative innovations has a limited half-life as their own cycle peaks. Only the early innovators will garner major success.

This is why *where we are in the cycle* joins emotion as the second major theme in my own speculative career.

SPECULATING IN THE STOCK MARKET – A SUMMATION

The key to my success in the stock market came only after finding in 1975 a strategy that both worked (made money) and fit my personality. By considering stocks only in industries that were undergoing a fundamental collapse, I needed to become comfortable with considering bad news and the resulting bad emotions that accompany collapsing stocks – fear, despair, anger – as an opportunity. This, as I have learned from books, experience, and my friend Rich Friesen, requires a personality shift for the typical investor. Included in the shift are factors like being alert to when my own emotions are telling me to make a change, such as aggressively selling a stock that I have become negative about (particularly when on margin), and alternatively aggressively buying a stock when greed tells me I have to own this one. Since I so seldom get this greedy, I end up being very concentrated in no more than three to five stocks and often only one major position (Coachman, Circuit City, or Huntsman). Another important tactic is to constantly be comparing the stocks I am in to other alternatives, so that a rising stock automatically pressures me to switch to one or more attractive alternatives. This has the shortcoming of missing the extended dramatic price increases of the best companies, but it is a shortcoming of my strategy I willingly accept.

A final aspect of my personality is curiosity. I am comfortable with the fact that had I continued to focus on speculating only in the US stock market and constantly honed the sharpness of my analysis (including crucially about where we were in the relevant cycles) I would be worth far more than I am, but I would have missed learning the ropes of speculating successfully in two other markets.

It is to the first of those two other markets – commodity futures – that we now will turn. But in order to explore commodity trading, let us first explore the third and last of the keys to my speculative success. The first was *emotion*, the second *was where are we in the cycle*, and now let me introduce the third – *illusion*. And let me introduce it by first describing an ancient society that more than any other was powered by illusion.

PART IV

THE FOURTH PIECE OF THE
MOSAIC

CHAPTER TEN

Byzantium – The Empire of Illusion

At the age of seven, upstairs in my Mill Valley, California, home, I came across the collected volumes of Ridpath's *History of the World – Being an Account of the Principal Events in the Career of the Human Race from the Beginning of Civilization to the Present Time*. I was drawn to Volume III, ROME. Initially I concentrated on the earlier days of Rome, but as time went on I became intrigued by what happened later with the rise of the Second Rome: Constantinople (now Istanbul), the capital of Byzantium.

What was it I found so intriguing about the Byzantine Empire? It was the ultimate survivor. Of all major empires, the Byzantine Empire was most practiced in the art of survival while on the strategic defensive. Time after time over its one-thousand-year history, its use of diplomacy was able to counter the larger armies of surrounding powers; its armory of diplomatic weapons was spectacular, consisting not merely of the five historical reliables – bribery, trade, assassination, alliances, and the threat of force – but also such innovative diplomatic weapons as clothing (most notably silk), titles, religion, language, and architecture.

The common theme of Byzantium's survival was the very conscious mastery of illusion – the ability to project the illusion of power as a complement to and, to an unique degree, a substitute for the reality of power.

One example was architecture. The architectural design of the Byzantine throne room was used to impress the barbarians (like those hot-headed French and English and Germans and Russians, who clearly lacked the sophistication of the Arab Caliphate to the East, to say nothing of the Byzantines themselves). Many of the barbarian foreigners invited to the throne room were puzzled by the lack of not only the emperor, but also the throne itself. And then, to their astonishment, they heard a roar of lions and, looking up, saw a massive throne descending from above with – yes, indeed – the emperor himself seated on the throne. And on each side of the throne were mechanical lions, roaring. A most impressive illusion of power a thousand years before the industrial revolution.

Byzantium was also famous for its art, especially the mosaic. The artist creates, via the placing piece by piece of small stones, the illusion of a portrait. Anyone can identify the portrait when all the stones are placed. But how about identifying the pattern whole when only a few of the stones are placed? That is the task of the successful speculator. That is the speculator's mosaic.

But Byzantium's use of illusion extended beyond art or architecture or diplomacy.

BYZANTIUM AND WAR

"Always mystify, mislead, and surprise the enemy, if possible."
~Stonewall Jackson

"All war is deception."
~Sun Tzu

In reading history, I quickly became an armchair general, learning about famous battles and great generals. And once again the history of the Byzantine Empire tracked a number of top generals. Just as the Byzantine diplomats were trained in the use of illusion, so too were the generals.

Byzantium was blessed with a number of first-rate generals who were also emperors, including Heraclius, Nicephorus Phocus, and Alexius Comneni. As emperors, they all controlled how big of an army they wished to lead. To see how powerful illusion can be in war, we turn to the greatest Byzantine general, Belisarius.

Limited by his emperor Justinian to a pitifully small army, Belisarius in 542 AD was sent to save the eastern frontier from another invasion by the enormous force of the Persian king Khusrow, who had already advanced into Byzantine territory west of the Euphrates river boundary. Rather than remaining on the defensive, Belisarius took his small army forward until they flanked the Persian army. This made Khusrow nervous because he felt that so great and victorious a general as Belisarius must have a huge army himself to be so bold. Seeking intelligence, Khusrow sent an ambassador to see Belisarius, ostensibly to discuss peace terms but really to verify how much of a threat the Byzantine army represented. So Belisarius took the most fearsome-looking half of this small army still further forward and dressed the men not for war, but for hunting game. Belisarius told the ambassador that he would be happy to discuss peace but only after Khusrow had retreated back across the river over the next five days. Convinced by Belisarius's illusions, Khusrow hastily retreated over the river and then negotiated a peace settlement with Belisarius.

And in reading about war, I came across B. H. Liddel Hart and *The Strategy of Indirect Approach*, which is described in Wikipedia thus:

> The indirect approach was a military strategy described and chronicled by B. H. Liddel Hart after World War I. It was Liddell Hart's attempt to find a solution to the problem of high casualty rates in conflict zones with high force-to-space ratios, such as the Western Front on which he served. The strategy calls for armies to advance along the line of least resistance. It is best described in this quote from his papers referring to the theory.

In battle, the longest way around is often the shortest way there. A direct approach to the object exhausts the attacker and hardens the resistance by compression, whereas an indirect approach loosens the defender's hold by upsetting his balance.

There were two fundamental principles that governed the indirect approach.

1. Direct attacks on firm defensive positions almost never work and should never be attempted.
2. To defeat the enemy, one must first disrupt his equilibrium. This cannot be an effect of the main attack; it must take place before the main attack is commenced.

Well, ever since, I have had a tendency as a speculator in venture capital to look for new young companies, particularly rank start-ups, that don't try to compete head-on against an incumbent provider (see my comment re: Henry J. Kaiser getting into the car market – or for that matter why I have been bearish on Tesla since 2015), but instead go around the competitor by coming up with something that in an important way is unique. (See my venture capital strategy – the Four Ds.)

Note that Byzantine diplomats when possible preferred the illusion of military power rather than going through the expense and uncertainty of actually giving battle. That was the last resort. The same was true for generals using the indirect approach. So, having learned at an early age how important illusion could be, I was primed to consider as a speculator to be aware of how illusions could be a powerful force that moved various markets (stock markets, bond markets, etc.).

THE ADVENT OF ILLUSION AND COMMODITY FUTURES

By now the reader understands that I place illusion alongside emotion and cycles as the third attribute I focus on for successful speculation. But how did I convert my historical interest in illusion into cold, hard cash?

While at Capital, all my individual speculative focus was on the American stock market. This changed one day in February of 1977, when one of the then junior analysts at Capital, Gregg Ireland, stepped into my office.

"Coffee," said Gregg quietly. "Come look." And we went into the Capital "war room" where all sorts of financial charts were kept updated on the wall for easy viewing and pondering. Sure enough, coffee in the commodity futures market had had a dramatic surge in price from about fifty cents per pound to over two dollars per pound. The reason for the rise was a severe freeze in Brazil in July of 1975 that had killed half of the coffee trees. The more I looked at this the more intrigued I got.

"Are you interested?" Greg asked.

"Yes," I said.

I'd been thinking of entering a second major market personally on top of the stock market. Why not commodity futures?

So I found a commodity futures broker in LA and opened an account, and Gregg and I partnered in going short coffee futures. The price at first went even higher, to over three dollars per pound in March 1977, but flush with my recent gains from Coachman, we met the margin calls.

Why, despite this being a new market, was I confident the price would come down? I had concluded the coffee market was entranced by *an illusion*, and primed by my knowledge of the power of Byzantine illusions, I was now ready to consider searching for illusion as a source of speculative profit.

The reigning illusion in early 1977 about the price of coffee was that because the cost of making a pot of coffee was so cheap, the demand for coffee would not be affected by the dramatic increase in price (economists call this "price inelastic") and therefore the high price would continue in the futures market. But I found counter information. I came across articles that said there had been a sudden change in American coffee consumption by putting less coffee grounds into the pot, making a weaker or a smaller pot of coffee. This change had happened suddenly and had not been predicted by the so-called coffee experts. After all, the price had quadrupled over the previous year with no discernable change in American consumption habits. But Gregg and I concluded that these new reports of American consumption drops would be enough, given time, to trigger a collapse in the price of our coffee futures, providing an example for what Malcolm Gladwell would later term a *tipping point*.

Coffee prices continued to surge past April Fool's Day of 1977, when I officially left Capital and moved north to San Francisco. On my way out the door, I was kindly serenaded by my Capital associates singing the "Capital Song" I had previously written. Gregg and I communicated by phone and resolved to hang in there by meeting margin calls. Fortunately, the tipping point came through within weeks. The price peaked at around $3.30 per pound and then began a dramatic decline. When the price crashed down to $1.80 in September 1977, we both cashed in and celebrated our win.

CHAPTER ELEVEN

The Emergence of Illusion

I look on my strategy for speculating in the stock market as largely unchanged since I first starting using it with Coachman in 1975. By contrast, my adventures in commodity futures have been less grounded. The major theme has been to look at all commodity futures opportunities (unlike the thousands of US stocks to pick from, the total number of commodity futures is small enough to track individually). Over 90 percent of commodity futures at any one time are neither extraordinarily high (as was coffee) nor extraordinarily low. My strategy is to ignore all of those commodities, going neither long nor short. I base my initial screen on "reversion to the mean" – the idea that when a price gets too high, it will *tend* to go down, and when a price gets too low, it will *tend* to go up. Part of the continuing development of my commodity futures strategy is based on reading in 1987 *The Alchemy of Finance* by George Soros, who cautions that reversion to the mean can sometimes be delayed interminably (i.e., prices can go much higher for much longer than one would think) because of the impact that investors have on prices and prices have on investors in the form of a feedback mechanism Soros calls "reflexivity."

Once I found a candidate for speculation, like going short on coffee, I would calculate how much of the total liquid net worth I would be prepared to *lose* on the speculation. The bets you can make in commodities are much bigger than those in stocks because you can put up a much smaller fraction of the value of the commodity. For example, I could short $100,000 worth of coffee by putting up no more than $5,000 to $10,000 in margin. Compare that with having to put up $50,000 or more to short $100,000 of any stock. So protecting oneself against major losses when you are so leveraged requires limiting your losses by putting in stop orders. To extend the example, if your liquid net worth was $200,000, and you were willing to risk 5 percent of that, then if you decided to short $500,000 worth of coffee, you would get out if coffee went up $10,000, or in this case 2 percent, and put in stops accordingly.

A critical feature that commodity futures trading has in common with trading stocks is that both are pure speculations with instant liquidity. No coffee bean or Folgers Coffee executive knew or cared that I was short a small number of coffee futures.

A second main feature of my early speculations in commodity futures was to consider them secondary or ancillary to my main speculations in stocks. My goal was to increase my liquid net worth by 10 percent per year from futures. I later had to change this concept when in the 1990s a time came where I stayed out of the stock market, meaning the sole liquid market I was speculating in was commodity futures.

My speculative instincts, whetted by the move into futures, were to expand further in the 1980s, and then I hit pay dirt indeed in 1990, courtesy of Saddam Hussein.

In 1990, the Iraqi leader, Saddam Hussein, invaded a small neighbor to the south, Kuwait. In the ensuing months, President Bush assembled a force to free Kuwait. Saddam Hussein, in an effort to abort the prospective United States military invasion, made a number of threats. A major threat was that if the United States invaded Kuwait or Iraq, Saddam would launch missiles against the Saudi Arabian oil fields and oil pipelines. The market, believing the seriousness of this threat, drove up the price of oil in the futures market, aided by numerous articles in the financial press that portrayed Saddam's threat to shut down oil production as credible.

As I read the press – not just the financial or energy press, but crucially the *military* press – I concluded that Saddam's threat was an empty one; that it was in fact an illusion. Why? Well, first, the military commentators said that Saddam's missiles were not accurate enough to hit either oil derricks or pipelines close enough to do much damage. Secondly, any damage to pipelines could be fixed in a short period of time. And thirdly, the Saudis had large quantities of oil stored in multiple locations, so they could continue a normal flow of oil exports for a considerable time just out of stored inventories. Fourthly, the massive (about 500,000 men) US military forces that were to lead the invasion were in northern Saudi Arabia, *between* Saddam's forces and the Saudi oil fields and pipelines to the south, meaning that the United States and the Saudi military could block any other attacks on the Saudi oil fields, including air strikes. Finally, Saddam, by using missiles, would risk an escalation of the conflict, justifying a United States missile counterstrike.

Therefore, I shorted oil futures shortly before the invasion date that President Bush had announced (actually, Bush gave Saddam a deadline on when he would have to start withdrawing his troops from Kuwait to avoid military action by the United States and its allies). The day after the invasion began, Saudi oil production remained inviolate, and Saddam's threats proved to be a bluff. Speculative Bob rubbed his greedy hands in triumph as the price of oil collapsed.

What this reinforced for me was that the markets are commonly deluded into giving credence to what are, on thorough examination, *illusions*. I had already come partway toward fading (i.e., betting on the opposite side) illusions before in my stock market strategy, which was based on looking for industries that were collapsing where, after thorough examination, I concluded that the industry would eventually come back. But now I would specifically look for illusions to bet against – in both commodity futures and the stock market.

THE PERSISTENCE OF ILLUSION

All illusions affecting the financial markets offer the opportunity to make money by speculating against them. But in determining how long the illusion can hold – that is, how persistent it is – I have not done a good job in assessing. The stock of Fannie Mae is a good example. I went short the stock in 2005 at $65 per share feeling that the government mandate to provide mortgages to people who were questionable payers was not going to end well for the company. And I was right, but two years too early, with the result that after twiddling my thumbs with the stock not breaking, I gave up. Had I continued to monitor the stock and been ready to re-short it when it broke below, say, $50 per share, all would have been well.

By contrast, when I shorted crude oil in 1990, correctly perceiving the fear that Saddam Hussein had the ability to knock out Saudi oil production was an illusion, I had a near-term deadline (when Bush was going to invade Iraq) that would expose the illusion and make me a significant profit when crude oil collapsed.

THE GOLDEN ERA

In 1993, the new Clinton Administration faced a major dilemma. They wanted to grow the economy, but doing this via the supply-side economics that had been successful under Reagan was out. Reagan's success was focused on cutting tax rates. By contrast, Clinton was locked into a policy of raising tax rates. But how could they stimulate the economy via traditional Keynesian stimulus without triggering fears of a replay of the 1970s, in which Keynesian stimulus and money printing led to roaring inflation and eventually spooked a collapse in the treasury bond market?

I concluded that the Clinton Administration solution, led by Treasury Secretary Robert Rubin, was to engineer a particularly massive illusion. The price of gold through history had been the best signal whenever a government debauched the currency. But what the Clinton Administration engineered (in cahoots with the European nations) was a coordinated series of public announcements from mostly European governments that they would sell into the open market large portions of their national gold reserves in one of two ways. Either they would sell directly into the market or in a less publicized manner lease physical gold to parties that would sell it into market. This net selling by various governments had never happened before because a nation's gold reserves had been looked on as a critical resource to be preserved and used only in time of emergency.

In the late 1990s, as the public gold selling continued, I became increasingly suspicious and looked for information. I subscribed to *LeMetropole Café* gold bug website, which I have found to be a valuable resource. The rationale pitched by the involved governments including the US for the gold sales was that a national country's gold just sat in the vault, earning nothing. By contrast, if the gold were sold, and the proceeds invested in, say, US Treasury bonds, then a significant safe income would be generated, and the country could expand its foreign aid spending to the impoverished world. But an additional impact of the sales was to allow the US to continue US spending, grow the US economy, and thereby aid foreign countries, including those selling their gold, to export more to the US, helping their own economies.

The process continued into the year 1999. The first of three events that year turned out to be the culmination of the process and the bottom in the price of gold. First, President Clinton and Treasury Secretary Rubin proposed that the IMF sell 10 percent of its gold. This proposal ran into trouble primarily because of opposition from the US Congress. Second, the British Labour government announced in July that it would sell 58 percent of its gold reserves over the ensuing three years. This announcement caused the gold price to drop about 10 percent to $252, which was its ultimate low. Finally, in September of 1999, the Washington Agreement on Gold was signed, under which a number of European central banks pledged to cap annual sales of gold at 400 tons. This announcement caused a rebound in the price of gold to about $300 per ounce.

Based on these three events, I concluded that gold and silver prices were artificially depressed and therefore buying gold and silver futures would pay off.

And boy, did they.

A WORD ON TAXES

I have focused on the importance of illusion as one of the keys in achieving successful speculation. In the broader world of politics, illusion is one of the chief weapons as we saw in the Byzantine Empire. And in no area of politics is illusion more important than in taxation.

When I was growing up in the 1950s, the economy was growing and the top rate on personal income taxes was 90 percent. Ever since, politicians on the left justify pushing for higher tax rates than the 37 percent of 2019 by pointing to the 1950s. Surely, they posit, such higher rates would generate more tax money for the government.

The Laffer Curve Lives: A 1950s Model

Assume an individual in the 1950s saw the prospect of earning $10 million. Thus, the politicians would think a return to the 90 percent top rate for individual income taxes would garner an extra $9 million for the government and leave the individual with $1 million. But would the reader be surprised to know that instead, almost every individual with such a prospect in the 1950s ended up not with $1 million but instead with $3.75 million? First, the individual would set up a corporation that would receive the $10 million per year (the corporate income tax in the 1950s was not 90 percent but 50 percent). Then, if the individual sold the corporation for its cash value – $5 million – she or he would have kept $3.75 million after taxes. Why? Because the third pillar of tax rates, capital gains, was only 25 percent.

This model shows the power of the Laffer Curve – the insight that if government sets the rate of tax too high (like a top rate of 90 percent), the government will end up not with more revenues, but *less*, as people learn how to legally avoid the punitive rates. US history bears that out, as the four times that there were major cuts in the personal income tax top rate – in the 1920s under Harding and Coolidge; in the 1960s under Kennedy and Johnson; and in the 1980s twice under Reagan in 1981/2 and 1986 – the economy responded with strong, low-inflation growth for at least the next three years.

For more info on the Laffer Curve, consult *The Way the World Works* by Jude Winnisky or *the Seven Fat Years* by Robert Bartley.

CHAPTER TWELVE
My Commodity Strategy

The basis of my speculating in commodity futures is reversion to the mean. Commodities differ from stocks in just that – being commodities. This means that when, for whatever cyclical reasons, there is a major surge in a commodity price (I like to see at least a triple), the odds are high that the price will collapse back. Collapse back to what? Collapse back to at least (and often below) the average mean price. Note that it is rare that any commodity is at such an extreme. But it is only those commodities that I consider, thus buying futures of commodities extremely low in price or selling futures of commodities extremely high in price. With every position I take, I calculate how much I am willing to risk (normally 1–2 percent of my liquid assets) and put in a stop order accordingly to limit my losses.

I have made much more money in the stock market and in venture capital. I typically think of commodity futures trading as an adjunct to my stock market speculations. In part because the number of plays in commodity futures is tiny compared with the stock market, the one time I did best in commodity futures was in the 2000–2008 period when I was out of the long side of the stock market and spending relatively little time in venture capital. My concentrating focus on commodity futures paid off in strong returns (primarily being long gold and silver futures).

I believe my speculative edge in commodity futures is smaller than that in either start-up venture capital or the stock market.

But although my speculative edge in commodity futures trading is smaller than in the stock market, it at least has been profitable overall. This has not been the case in my later experiences with the game that initiated my life as a speculator. But I promise that once I detail my recent career in poker, I will shift to my final and very different form of speculation: venture capital.

POKER REDUX

After graduating from college in 1965, I took a breather from poker. But the breather ended when I enrolled at a business school near Boston, on the Charles River. I was sitting in my school section – Section E – when a Texan stopped by my desk.

"I hear you play poker," John Keller said.

I admitted that I played the game.

"Well, we're putting together a game tonight in McCulloch Lounge at seven p.m."

"I'll be there."

Now, the players in this game were fellow students at Harvard Business School. But to a veteran of the Cameo Club, they were juicy fish. With one exception: John Keller. John watched as I gutted more than one poor student, sending him away muttering. Finally, John had had enough. He invited me to get a meal across the river. We ended at Elsie's, where John laid out some of the facts of poker.

"Now, Leppo, it's obvious that you and I are going to be the only ones making money at the game, but you are hammering these fish so hard that some of them won't come back. If you take things a little slower, we'll both make more money over the long term."

I agreed readily to take his advice (after all, I had noticed that a couple of my new friends had attended our game once but had not returned).

There had been, for example, a student from Greece who so loved to play in our little game that he had on more than one occasion had funds wired from home.

As a youth in East Texas, John Keller had started playing extensive poker in a few private games with grown men and had learned how to win without breaking up the game. And on the Charles, he won at least twice as much as I did. As a married student, the poker game provided an important supplement to his income. In short, John had a background as a professional poker player whereas I was an amateur, as could be seen in how John was careful to keep our Greek friend a happy player.

What I learned from this is, in any field, to know the difference between the professionals and the amateurs and defer to the professionals.

I soon refined *professional* to *world class*. I developed two tests to separate those who claimed to be world class at something – but were not – from those who actually were world class.

- Test number one: Ask both a question concerning their field they are unlikely to know the answer to. The one answering "I don't know" is world class.
- Test number two: Ask both to talk about their field. The one delighted to talk – and at length – is world class.

2003 AND THE MONEYMAKER EFFECT

So this kid Chris Moneymaker came out of nowhere to win the biggest tournament in poker in 2003. I watched him play on TV and said to myself, "I can do that." The next week I went into a local poker casino – Artichoke Joe's – and played my first hand of Texas Hold 'Em poker.

My return to poker in 2003 was for very different reasons than my earlier forays in the game. When I played in college at the Cameo Club, poker was my main focus as a budding speculator. The money I made was important money to me. But in 2003, other areas of speculation were where the money was to be made (or lost). Instead, my new interest in poker was as a mental exercise. Having just turned sixty, I wanted to maintain my edge longevity-wise. On the physical side, this featured connecting with a four-times-per-week personal trainer. But playing regular poker at casinos near San Francisco has provided a mental exercise regimen where the speculative wins or losses provide a critical discipline. The three fundamentals of my personal speculative tactics – emotion, illusion, and cyclicality – are all present, but the use of those tactics is compressed into seconds or at most minutes. As is the case with any area of speculation, there is always more to learn and, most importantly, more to learn about myself.

Poker had changed from the collegiate glory days at the Cameo Club where I started winning almost immediately. Texas Hold 'Em is a far more complicated game.

In Texas Hold 'Em, each player is dealt two cards face down (which only the player sees); there is then a round of betting. All subsequent cards are dealt face up and available to every player to use in making their best hand. The first three cards dealt face up are called *the flop*, and there is a second round of betting. Then a fourth card is dealt called *the turn*, and a third round of betting. Finally, a fifth and final card is dealt called *the river*, and a fourth round of betting ensures, after which all cards are revealed and the best five-card poker hand takes the pot.

At Artichoke Joe's, I played in their smallest game and lost steadily for a couple weeks (maybe $1,000 in all) before saying to myself once again: "You speculator you, you need a strategy." I bought the first of many poker books on Texas Hold 'Em. This was by Phil Hellmuth, and it outlined a beginning strategy that I adopted. Almost immediately, I started breaking even at the smallest game. But as I moved up to the next-smallest game, I started losing again as the competition kept getting better. As a result, I chocked up losses of over $200,000 while learning the game. Since developing my strategy of poker, I make consistent money playing smaller games, tend to lose when I get into the toughest games, and roughly break even overall.

Starting with 2004, I have averaged playing about three hours per day. Once again, as in each other market in which I have speculated, the knowledge of and successful manipulation of emotion is a key to success.

The most important aspect of emotion you need to master is dealing with losses that are substantial, unavoidable, and unlucky. In poker, this is called *the bad beat*. As you will read, I focus a lot on emotion in all the areas I speculate in, but poker is different in terms of time. The pace is fast in that within seconds after losing a hand because another player got grossly lucky on the River, guess what: you have to play the next hand.

CHAPTER THIRTEEN

The Emergence of CHELP

After considerable effort, the guts of my strategy in playing Texas Hold 'Em is the acronym CHELP.

- **C**-ombinatrics
- **H**-arrington
- **E**-motion
- **L**-ook
- **P**-lan

With every hand I play, I keep CHELP in mind.

C FOR COMBINATORICS

Combinatorics is a term from poker authors Tri Nguyen and Cole South. It refers to combinations of hands in Texas Hold 'Em. Often in a hand when figuring out whether to call another player's bet, you are puzzling over which of several types of hands this player may have.

Consider a hand where you have 99 and the board was 9 8 3 2 ... and the final (river) card was a 6. You with your top three of a kind or set make a bet, and the other player makes a very large raise.

If I think the only hands that could cause such a big raise are either the smaller sets 88, 66, 33, 22 (all of which I beat), or a straight (to which I lose), what should I do?

The answer is: consult combinatorics and compare the possible combinations of hands that you can beat (the smaller sets) with the possible combinations of the straights to which you lose. First the sets: if the 7 on the board is the 7 of clubs, then your opponent must have either 7 of spades and hearts or 7 of spades and diamonds or 7 of hearts and diamonds – that is a total of three combinations, meaning there are a total of twelve combinations for all four of the sets. By contrast, both of the straight possibilities 7 and 10, as well as 7 and 5, have sixteen combinations. Since there are only twelve combinations I can beat, whereas there are thirty-two combinations I lose to, I fold my hand.

H FOR HARRINGTON

The great poker player Dan Harrington in his books *Harrington on Cash Games I and II* teaches that whenever a player makes a bet, the question you ask yourself is, "What are the chances that that specific player made that bet with a hand my hand can beat?" You fold unless the chance you will win is close to how much is in the pot. For example, there is $100 in a pot and you think your hand has a 25 percent chance of winning. If the other player bets $50, you call, but if he bets $150, you fold.

One of the keys to the benefit of Harrington's tactic is that it forces you to consider the various possible hands your opponent might have rather than try to put the opponent on a specific hand (as many poker players do).

E FOR EMOTION

I find in all the markets I speculate in, including poker, that understanding emotion is critical.

My Own Emotion

In poker, the most important emotion I have to deal with is my own frustration, either the frustration at having lost a big hand or series of smaller hands or the frustration of an extended period of time (in my case, over two or three hours) of getting consistently lousy starting cards, thus getting bored with throwing away hand after hand. The second and related emotional trap is when after a long period of lousy cards I finally get a very good starting hand (either AA or KK or QQ) and I build a good-size pot partway through the hand. But when another player makes a significant bet against me, rather than folding as I would in normal circumstances, having "unemotionally" followed Dan Harrington's advice, instead I get so caught up in the hope that finally this hand can win me a big pot that I stay with the hand and end up making a major loss.

Benefitting From the Emotions of Other Players

Many poker players play carefully, only continuing with hands that have considerable strength. These players (called *nits*, in poker parlance) are emotionally uncomfortable being deceptive. This discomfort manifests itself in ways that us poker players call a *tell*. For example, I save a lot of money by folding to a nit who makes even a medium-sized bet. Other players with emotional states different from the cautious nits have correspondingly different tells. In becoming aware of tells, I have learned most from Mike Caro's *Caro's Book of Poker Tells*. I find that the bigger the game and the more skilled the players, the greater is the benefit of focusing on the tells for each player at the table.

After Three Hours

Typically, after a session lasts over three hours, I often notice my emotional state changing toward boredom if I have no exciting hands, toward frustration if I am losing via repeated unlucky hands, or just toward impatience. When I notice such increasing emotions, I end the session.

The Next Emotional Layer

Having considered my own emotional state and the emotional state of the other players, the final layer to consider is what the other players think of you. I am an old white guy. In general, other poker players assume that old white guys are nits. I try to foster that impression to my benefit. If I win two pots from a folding player, I will often show the hand where I had him or her beat but never show the bluff. On the other hand, if I am caught bluffing and have to show my hand, I will make sure the whole table knows that I bluffed and then for a period of time (perhaps an hour max) do no bluffing to re-establish my nit image.

L FOR LOOK

Because I am hard of hearing, I do a poor job of picking up tells from what players are saying. Instead, I concentrate on looking for visual clues. The most important of these is how the player bets. This again is a subject well covered by Mike Caro. One factor for me is that I play so much poker at the same few casinos that I know on sight all the good players.

Another reason for emphasizing looking is that I often read while at the poker table. While this helps me avoid the boredom that can lead to frustration and poor play, I miss whatever is happening visually while I've got my nose buried in a newspaper. In this case, I think I gain more from reducing boredom than I lose by limiting my looking.

P FOR PLAN

One of the best aggressive players I know thinks that planning is the key to winning poker.

For most players, myself included, when they pick up their two cards, they immediately know, most of the time, that they will fold. No planning required. Such automatic action called *thinking fast* is detailed in *Thinking, Fast and Slow* by Daniel Kahneman. The more poker I play, the greater the percent of hands I can make the right decision on when thinking fast. And thereby lies the problem. You definitely benefit from planning rather than thinking fast when you're in the biggest hand of the night with your entire stack on the line. My best decisions about any hand require taking the time to consciously and deliberately review and then plan – that is, think slow. In poker, thinking slow to plan normally takes me ten to thirty seconds.

In the first phase of any hand, when all the players have are their two concealed cards, whether or not I take the time to plan depends largely on position. If I am one of the first to act and therefore in early position and I have a poor hand, then folding without planning is reasonable. But often when in late position, I need to plan before folding even a poor hand.

For example, if a nit has made a small bet and a very aggressive player has raised and my image at this particular table is that I am a nit too, it may make sense for me to re-raise.

But it is when the flop comes down that planning is most profitable. As I play more and more Texas Hold 'Em, I can make a greater and greater percentage of correct decisions while thinking fast.

But so what?

Remember that your entire stack can be wiped out with just one snap decision. And the same caution applies to the last parts of the hand: the turn and the river.

I use a tactic to encourage planning. Whenever I catch myself losing a big pot through lack of planning, I institute my tactic. I get up from the table and end the session. I have the choice of either playing no more for that day or playing but only in a smaller game. By contrast, as long as I make no bad decisions, I can keep playing even if I suffer losses from bad cards.

For more info, I recommend any Hold 'Em books authored by Dan Harrington or Ed Miller.

WITH CHELP IN HAND – MY FINAL THOUGHTS ON POKER

Since of the four markets in which I speculate, poker is the smallest, it does not matter financially whether I win or lose.

The main reason I play poker is that it is a form of mental exercise. I enjoy the discipline of trying to improve, and for me the key area for me to improve is in psychology: specifically, doing a constantly better job of making good decisions based on understanding of my own and each of the other players' emotional states.

Time and geography matter. In every casino in which I have repeatedly played Hold 'Em, I find the quality of the competition is constantly growing, and the games are getting tougher and tougher over time. The three cities where the games are toughest are San Francisco, Los Angeles, and Las Vegas.

When I notice that I am getting tired or bored, I quit for the day.

Remember the old saying: *there is more to poker than life*.

PART V

THE MOSAIC COMES

TOGETHER

CHAPTER FOURTEEN
Venture Capital

Of the four speculative arenas I have fought in, three of them – poker, the stock market, and commodity futures – differ significantly from the fourth: start-up venture capital. In the first three, your role is one of an observer of reality, whereas in the fourth, you are a participant in creating a new reality. The most useful preparation for moving away from pure speculation into the complexities of start-ups I learned from my historical mentor, Andrew Carnegie.

The book about Carnegie that I most recommend is the biography *Andrew Carnegie* by Joseph Frazier Wall. Like myself, Carnegie parleyed the money he saved from his salary as a full-time employee into a series of speculations in various start-ups, including some wild speculations in the Pennsylvania oil fields. Even more important, Carnegie never sought to be CEO of any of his ventures. Carnegie had much more operating chops than I ever did, particularly in terms of sales, investment banking, and business development. But overall, I resonated most from how Carnegie succeeded in business primarily as an investor rather than an operator.

I should add that the true operators I read about that have taught me the most memorable lessons just below include J. D. Rockefeller, James J. Hill, Henry Ford, E. H. Harriman, Ray Kroc, and Steve Jobs. I particularly recommend, re: Jobs, *The Little Kingdom* by Michael Moritz.

This reading, plus my earlier successful development of a strategy for stock market speculation, convinced me that as I "ventured" into this new (to me) arena, I would need to come up with a strategy that would work and also fit my personality. I came up with something very different, and it has turned out to be the most financially successful of all.

THE FIRST VENTURE: C. D. ANDERSON

In 1979, I got a call from Derek Anderson, a schoolmate and senior partner of the stock brokerage firm C. D. Anderson. Derek asked if I would buy some equity in his firm, which I was comfortable doing, in part because all my assets were liquid and the sum was a relatively small investment of $10,000. I knew nothing about venture capital (other than what I had read) but was already wise enough to at least not make a pest of myself as a minority investor.

In 1982, I got a check for over $100,000 from Derek when C. D. Anderson was sold.

Just as with coffee and commodity futures, my first venture capital foray was very profitable. My interest in venture capital was whetted.

THE HIPPIE IN THE SPORTING GOODS STORE

In 1978, I was in a Mill Valley sporting goods store to pick up some tennis balls, and I noticed that the long-blond-haired hippie cashier selling me the tennis balls was also checking out my *Forbes* magazine, then owned by Malcolm Forbes.

"Oh, Malcolm," he said. That snapped me out of my reverie and started a friendship, including playing tennis together with Jim Harleen.

I started spending time with Jim and his fiancée, Stephanie DiMarco, both recent college graduates. Stephanie was interested in business and finance and ended up working for a series of money managers. In one case, she was the bookkeeper for a money manager who specialized in selling options, mostly naked calls, and pocketing the premiums. One day, Stephanie heard a takeover bid for one of the stocks her boss had written calls on. Stephanie instantly calculated that the firm was now busted, totally. Stephanie agreed – if paid in advance – to help the poor guy close down his firm, which included remaining calm and professional as one angry client after another stormed through the office door.

And then Stephanie worked for the Marin money manager, Kit Cole, who had at the time a sticker on the back of her car reading "So Many Men, So Little Time."

Stephanie, as a part of her work, knew that keeping automated accounting of investment portfolios required expensive mini computer hardware and also expensive time-sharing bureaus. But in that year, 1983, Stephanie noticed that the IBM PC could keep track of portfolio accounting for much less cost if – and only if – a genius programmer could create a new system that was built for the PC.

And Stephanie also knew that just such a genius programmer, Steve Strand, was working alongside her as a software consultant for Ms. Cole. Stephanie heard opportunity knocking. But Steve Strand could only go full time on the project if his mortgage was paid. So Stephanie had to find an investor.

"Bob," Stephanie said earnestly, "I can do this if I can get an investor for fifty thousand."

By chance, I had just gotten very flush from the surge in Wards, a.k.a. Circuit City. So I said, "What do I get for my fifty thousand?"

"How about six percent?" said Stephanie instantly, nodding and smiling.

"More," I managed to say.

"Ten percent," said Stephanie, nodding and smiling more vigorously.

Finally, I nodded. "OK."

I should say that Stephanie at her young age was already more polished in business negotiation than I will ever be. By her suggesting the valuation, starting out with a low figure so that even a modest increase in my share was still a very good deal for her, she achieved a real coup and started Advent Software while giving up only 10 percent of the equity for the crucial money.

PLUNGING DEEPER INTO VENTURE

In 1983, I plunged into venture capital with three investments, Advent Software being one and Information America being the second. The bulk of my investment went into Information America; the bulk of the profits came from Advent.

Why was Advent so much more successful? Three factors stand out.

1. Information America entered a market (providing state government information primarily to corporate law firms) where well-funded competition already existed. By contrast, Advent Software planned to build the very first software for money-management firms that could run on an IBM PC rather than needing a mini-computer time-sharing system. When you are

     a start-up, staying away from direct and entrenched competition via importantly unique features is a big help. But I didn't appreciate that in 1983.

2.   Management structure. Advent had a clear line of authority. Stephanie DiMarco became CEO. By contrast, Information America had two CEOs. This led to confusion in my mind about who was responsible for various aspects of the company.

3.   Me. I thought that as a seasoned speculator and lead investor (well, with Advent I was the only investor), I would surely come up with a series of *helpful* suggestions that would improve the company. Management reacted differently to my suggestions. The Information America management (knowing that they might well need more of my money) tried to accommodate my suggestions, such as opening a branch sales office to serve a smaller market that intrigued me. This suggestion of mine turned out to be both wrong and expensive. By contrast, Stephanie at Advent (who crucially got to positive cash flow after only six months) would listen carefully to all my suggestions but had no problem in winnowing out those she felt did not measure up. The ideas that Stephanie found of most value all came from one friend, Reece Duca. Reece's Santa Barbara firm became one of Stephanie's early customers. Next, Stephanie used first as consultant and then board member Reece's close ally, the marketing expert Frank Robinson. Finally, Reece and his younger partner Tim Bliss provided extensive oversight as well as investment, culminating in Reece agreeing to become chairman of Advent.

CHAPTER FIFTEEN

Launching into Disaster

And now came my third 1983 venture investment. Flush with my profits from Circuit City, I went to a conference on aerospace and met Gary Hudson. A self-taught aerospace engineer, Gary had designed the first privately funded rocket, which had exploded on the launchpad in 1981. He wanted to raise $300 million to build a new launch vehicle. Intrigued, I invested $10 thousand for 1983, 1984, and 1985. Then in 1986, the *Challenger* disaster happened, and President Reagan announced that the federal government's launch needs would now be open to riding on privately developed rockets. I called Gary and asked what this meant. He said he could now get into the rocket business with $30 million rather than $300 million. I responded that if he could move his need down an order of magnitude from nine figures ($300 million) to eight ($30 million), I could move up my funding from five figures ($10 thousand) to six (hundreds of thousands).

I was captured by a vision of myself throwing a satellite into space (I had remembered the first scene from the movie *2001: A Space Odyssey*), and for the next seven years, I was more captured by the vision of helping to get man into space than any other venture I had been involved in before. And that emotion drove me to work harder to make a venture happen than anything I had done up to that point.

Gary Hudson first opened an office and next got a government contract to build an engine. Then I reached out to a friend, Tom Barry, for more funding, which I largely guaranteed. And then Gary's venture – Pacific American Launch Systems – lost the key Pentagon rocket engine contract and ran out of money.

Nothing daunted despite having to sell some of my Advent stock to pay off my guarantee, I transferred my rocket loyalty to a new CEO that Gary Hudson introduced me to as a contact. Rick Fleeter, the founder and CEO of a growing and profitable small satellite company AeroAstro, agreed to take on where Gary left off, and so Rick founded and I funded a new rocket company, this time called PacAstro. PacAstro also got a government contract re: the engine. But once again (we are now up to 1993), more money was needed. I pledged to invest $2 million in this venture and sought to raise the money by selling another portion of my Advent software stock.

At this point, reality interceded. I was not allowed to sell any Advent stock. The totally appropriate reason was that Advent, in order to hold down the price of new employee options, did not want a new sale of stock at a higher price.

Result: I was stymied and shaken to my business core.

ROCKET MISTAKES

What mistakes did I make in my foray into the rocket business?

Let me count the ways:

I was overcome by emotion. When the *Challenger* went down, I had a vision of myself as helping Gary Hudson and his rocket-building team lift mankind toward the stars.

Advent Software was already a major venture capitalistic success. Surely, I thought (or better yet *felt*), I could expand on that success in the rocket field.

I had no experience in raising funding, but I mistakenly thought that the speculative success I was known for among my circle of friends would stimulate them to invest.

Most critically, I had yet to develop any skill in figuring out how my limited investment could get a start-up venture to positive cash flow with the bare minimum amount of funding.

And the key mistake was that of self-sacrifice. By committing increasingly larger portions of my liquid assets to the rocket business, I opened myself up to massive business stress. This stress, which lasted for the second half of 1993, was cumulative, resulting in a tingling of my prostate – wow!

What did I do? I called Arkansas, of course.

ARKANSAS PILGRIMAGE

On that day in December, 1993, Dr. Ted Morter picked up the phone in Rogers, Arkansas. When I explained my situation, he replied, "Well, you better get down here."

After four weeks in Arkansas, with key help from Dr. Morter, I both hit bottom and started the road back.

I had been to see Dr. Morter before as a result of the decline in my hearing from 1971 to 1985. By that time, I was forced to wear hearing aids and finally agreed, under the care of tinnitus expert Dr. Paul Yannick, to shift my diet to vegan (no animal products). This began to work, particularly in terms of improving my ability to understand speech. When I was to go back to see Dr. Yannick in New Jersey, he called me and said I should meet him instead in Arkansas and meet Dr. Morter, a chiropractor and developer of the Morter Health System's program called Bio Energetic Synchronization Technique, or B.E.S.T.

What is B.E.S.T.? Here is the explanation from the Morter Health System website:

> B.E.S.T. is a non-forceful, energy-balancing, hands-on procedure used to help reestablish the full healing potential of the body. Understanding the body makes no mistakes regarding health and longevity, B.E.S.T. principles acknowledge the concept of Interference we create with our conscious mind. This Interference caused imbalance in the autonomic nervous system leading to exhaustion of our organ systems over time. Researched at major universities, taught in several Chiropractic Colleges and in professional continuing education seminars, B.E.S.T. is recognized as an effective healing science. The principles and concepts of Morter Health System and B.E.S.T. technique are available to families, therapists, and health care practitioners.

The five weeks I spent at Dr. Morter's home, often sitting by the fireplace talking, saved my life. How? By teaching me how to control my own emotions by adjusting as needed the core beliefs that were triggering my emotional response.

One of the key examples Dr. Morter taught me was the story of the caveman walking along the jungle path and meeting a tiger. As Dr. Morter explained, the body responds perfectly to that event by having the negative emotion of fear pump up adrenaline, and within a few minutes, one of three outcomes happens: you run away from the tiger, you fight the tiger and win, and then the third outcome. But in all three cases, the need for the negative emotion to trigger the adrenaline is over and done with, and so the adrenaline quickly disappears once the crisis is over. But what if you are a modern caveman working in an office and the tiger is your boss? Or in my case, what if the tiger was my own self-imposed commitment to fund a rocket company? A commitment that fueled my negative emotions and therefore my adrenaline response, but a commitment I was powerless to fulfill.

And that's what I learned at that fireplace: how to beneficially shift my emotions to respond with positive emotions to whatever past experience or present dilemma was damaging me.

THE IMPORTANCE OF THE MORTER TECHNIQUE FOR THE SPECULATOR

There were several advances in speculation I made once I thoroughly learned the Morter B.E.S.T. technique. First and most important, I learned how to reverse the symptoms of stress that so concerned me. Specifically, I was getting symptoms in my prostate of tingling and pain whenever I thought about my main business dilemma at the time. I had pledged to Rick Fleeter to invest money in PacAstro but was barred from raising it by selling Advent stock.

A second and related benefit was that I became more alert to negative emotions, so that when those emotions were tied to a speculation (i.e., I owned a stock that I noticed I was nervous about), I treated those negative emotions *immediately*, using Morter techniques in such a way that I *always* resolved them so that they no longer had any impact on my emotional state. Third, I started (this is still not something I am very good at) to be aware of how negative emotions can damage me as a speculator. The most important of these is the emotion of complacency. This is particularly damaging because, as I have admitted here previously, I have a strong tendency toward laziness. I can cite multiple examples of this damaging duo (complacency coupled with laziness) that have occurred when I invested in a position that went my way (became quite profitable) in a short period of time. All too often, I did not foresee that the prices and profits could reverse because I was too lazy to continue to update my research/opinion of the speculation based on the change in price. This was also tied to being lazy in not keeping the table comparing potential percentage gains over the ensuing eighteen months that I had used in the 1970s.

In my daily life, the most important tactic I learned from Morter is how to use prayer to immerse myself in positive rather than negative emotions. Every day I say the class of prayer (or mantra if you will) I learned at B.E.S.T., such as:

> *Thank you, Lord, for this wonderful life.*
> *Thank you, Lord, for my wonderful body.*
> *Thank you, Lord, for this beautiful day.*
> *Thank you, Lord, for my wonderful friends.*

Anyone interested in learning more should check out one of Morter's books, particularly *Dynamic Health*. In addition, you could consider attending one of his seminars. You can find out more at https://www.morter.com/events/.

CHAPTER SIXTEEN
The Internet Changes Everything

I got a call in late 1994 from David Buzby. "Want to consider investing in an ISP?" he asked.

"Sure," I replied. "But what is an ISP?"

"Internet Service Provider. They allow you to hook up your personal computer to the Internet. You've heard of the Internet?"

"I think so."

"Bob, they're growing really fast and they need money. If you like it, I might take an offer to become the CFO."

So Buzby and I arrived at the Silicon Valley headquarters of Best Internet. They had opened up six months before and had gotten one thousand customers the first month, each paying $29.95 per month for dial-up access, combined with something called a website. A key to Best's success was that since getting on and using the early Internet was complicated, a customer could bring in his personal computer to the Best office and Best would set the customer up. This had proved to be a marketing coup.

I invested what I could and went on the board. Why? Because the revenue growth rate from a standing start was overwhelmingly compelling, and I was already aware of how quickly the Internet was growing.

Being the lead investor in Best was a great ride that ended when the company was first combined with another ISP, HiWay, then sold to Verio. But although I remained in my normal speculative role as the outside lead investor, I did have an impact on the company's success largely via my involvement in venture office politics.

VENTURE OFFICE POLITICS: IN PREPARATION FOR BEST INTERNET

Prior to investing in Best, I had read about the most memorable masters of office politics. I don't like to engage in it myself, but sometimes it is unavoidable. Here are a couple of mistakes I made in venture investing that prepared me for my more successful forays into the field.

Information America

In one of my early venture investments, Information America, I pressured management at one of our quarterly board of director meetings to enter a small market in Texas. Information America's customers were mostly corporate law firms, and while at the time management was entering the two largest concentrations of lawyers in Houston and Dallas, I felt that the lawyers practicing in Austin and neighboring San Antonio, when combined, would be a profitable enough market to have a salesperson stationed there. Management buckled, largely because the company was losing money and wanted to keep their lead investor (that would be me) sweet. The result: the new salesman, after considerable effort and expense, was let go. On top of that, Lord knows how much top management time was wasted in buttering up the lead investor (that would be me).

Oops!

Since that negative experience in office politics, while I continue to give advice to entrepreneurs/CEOs, I never seek to make any operating decisions myself regardless of how much stock in the venture I own. This is primarily because I have no successful experience in operating any company myself. Once I became self-employed and tried any operating role, I immediately missed being able to lie in bed and read the latest book on the Byzantine Empire.

Advent Software

I had assured the founder and CEO of Advent, Stephanie DiMarco, that I would back her as CEO. But when the co-founders of Advent had conflicting visions of how the software should be developed, and Stephanie decided the best solution was to buy out the other founder, Steve Strand, I intervened by openly encouraging Steve not to sell out.

Note that the two co-founders owned the same amount of Advent stock so that in the case of disagreement, my vote would be deciding. Even though in the end I supported the buy-out, I delayed and complicated the whole process. Since that experience, I always in a similar situation would, once a disagreement arose, get together with the CEO and resolve my concerns so that we would present a united front on the issue. In the case of Advent, had I coordinated better with Stephanie, I could have encouraged her to push for a deal whereby Steve, while selling most of his stock (80 or even 90 percent), would have retained enough to benefit from the future success of the company.

The way I describe my goal in such a situation is to say:

When one of two co-founders wants to buy out the other, I always recommend that the selling founder be left with a portion – say ten percent. That way, whenever I walk down the street, I am happy to meet whoever I have done business with coming the other way, including the selling co-founder.

With that political preparation, let us turn to Best Internet. In 1994, I invested in Best Internet, one of the pioneer Internet service providers (ISPs) and a true pioneer in the web-hosting industry. Three times in two years I was asked by the CFO to be involved with the office politics of bringing in a new CEO. I did the best job in engineering the third and final change. Why? Because already I had learned some lessons at Best.

BEST INTERNET: LESSONS LEARNED

The most important lesson that Best reinforced was that fast growth covers a multitude of sins; whenever I hear of a private venture whose revenue is growing quickly (annual growth rate of over 50 percent), I become *very* interested. Of course, I had already learned this lesson from public companies, most notably the turnaround at Coachman and the start-up surge at Advent.

A second lesson was the awareness of how fast-growing ventures stress the ability of the original entrepreneur to adapt and grow.

When I invested in Best, I recalled what my classmate and eventual business partner Mark Ludwig told me about what his management consulting background taught him about fast-growing companies. Mark told me that each time a company's revenue triples, the role of a CEO changes. Up to $1 million in annual revenues, the CEO can be a one-man or -woman show. But in order to get to the $3 million level, the CEO has to start to delegate important aspects of the business to others. This means he or she has to let go not of ultimate authority but rather ultimate knowledge. Increasingly, there will be others who know more about important aspects of the company than he or she does. Those CEOs that resist this delegating process cause their company to stagnate. The following phase of getting the company past $3 million and up to around $10 million (another triple) requires another kind of delegation: delegating leadership. Increasingly, the employees who report to the CEO are managing teams of their own or projects of their own. If the CEO fails to provide those managers with the authority to manage, once again, stagnation can result. And so it goes. Mark's management consulting background has been invaluable in counseling CEOs in navigating the company through these growth phases or alternatively bringing in new leadership.

A third lesson was the importance of getting and staying in positive cash flow. After all, the great venture capitalist Arthur Rock would give out T-shirts to start-up CEOs that said *HAPPINESS IS POSITIVE CASH FLOW*. Unfortunately, much of the early leadership of Best were captured by the vision that spending to fuel growth was more important than positive cash flow. The losses in pushing growth became a critical issue to me, since in my excitement I had cashed out my Advent and transferred most of the money to an increased investment in Best. (This was my Dr. Johnson moment.) David Buzby as Best CFO tugged at his lead investor (that would be me) with increasing urgency. And I was ready to help because I had learned from my Best experience who to call in Las Vegas.

THE EMERGENCE OF ZARLEY

I had met Jim Zarley in 1986, when he was a senior executive at Quantech, a publicly traded stock I had invested in. I was instantly impressed with his knowledge of the art of operations. In evaluating a company's leader, I would often ask myself if I would want to work for this person. I quickly put Jim near the top of the list. (The idea was only theoretical, mind you, as I preferred the speculator's independence.) Within three years, Jim acquired a division of Quantech, making the entrepreneurial leap. He built it up and sold it for enough to be able to move to Nevada to focus on real-estate investing.

I visited him in Las Vegas, and he mentioned a storage investment he had considered in there. "I decided not to buy the deal. They had told me there were 560 storage units, but in fact there were only 554."

"Jim, how did you know?" I asked.

"I counted them," Jim replied.

We kept in touch, so once I invested in Best I invited him to take a look. Jim did come up to see Best, was instantly impressed with David Buzby, but overall remained cautious about getting involved.

Meanwhile, once Best started losing money, I ramped up my calls to Las Vegas until eventually I heard Jim say:

"Bob, in the past when you asked if I would get involved in Best, I always said no. If you were to ask again, I would say yes."

So I got to work (office politics) to bring Mr. Zarley into Best. But the key to my success in getting Jim into Best was in letting Jim lead the process.

Six Lessons from Zarley

One. Best at the time had a seven-person board, of which I was only one member and the only one who knew Jim. Convincing a majority of the board to replace the current CEO (who did not want to leave) was therefore tricky. Why? Because the company had already had three CEOs, and the board of directors – made up of the largest individual (angel) investors – was cautious about once again making a major change. Jim accomplished his takeover via a three-part strategy. First, he offered to start not as CEO but rather as a consultant who was in charge of the budget. Second, before long, the current CEO, seeing that the budget was going to be changed against his liking (Jim's changes including an immediate sharp cut in marketing costs), offered to resign. Finally, Jim offered to work as CEO for three months for no compensation, thus giving the board time to see how Jim performed before getting locked into any deal.

Two. When Jim Zarley took command at Best, he called a meeting of employees and addressed them as follows: "I think the most important thing about working at a company is to have fun, but it's tough to have fun when you are losing money." Zarley's use of the word *fun* was deliberate. As Jim says, "Having a history in doing turnarounds, one of my first actions is to call a meeting of all the employees and explain why it is necessary to make some immediate changes in the way we do business. Most people are very logical and usually well aware of the problems. They appreciate the candor, and it makes them a part of the solution. My pledge to them as employees is never to allow their jobs to be put at risk again. This pledge is also made to investors and shareholders."

This explains why getting any company losing money to positive cash flow is Jim's (and Mark Ludwig's) number one priority. It is also mine. I should note that during the bubble phase of the Internet (1993– 2000), many companies downplayed getting to profitability – in many cases yielding to the cyclical fad of focusing on other priorities, such as, "You need to get big fast," or "What counts in the Internet is not profitability but growth in traffic," or "What counts in the Internet is not profitability but dominating a space."

Profitability, cash, and assets (particularly saleable assets) are the reality of value specifically because they are an insurance policy against bankruptcy.

Three. Whenever Jim concluded that he had to let an employee go, he would get together with the employee privately and often start the conversation with the phrase, "It's time to move on." Jim found that phrase particularly useful because, "by the time you have exhausted every possibility to help an employee to meet your expectations with no success, they are as ready to leave as you are for them to go. With this in mind, the decision is easier and can usually be done by mutual agreement."

Four. When Jim needed to cut back the size of a company he was running, he always made the cutback big enough so the company would immediately be back in positive cash flow. This allowed him to document to the remaining employees that their jobs were safe. Jim feels that "understanding how much cost needs to be taken out of a turnaround is crucial. Cut just one time. There's nothing worse than death by a thousand cuts."

Five. Jim also emphasizes the need to "share the company's success stories with the employees and make them a part of the financial turnaround. Establish regular meetings sharing successes and the direction the company is going."

Six. In this lesson, Jim was a conduit for his friend Earle Malm. Earle states that there are four and only four things you need to say to any friend that should *never* be put off:

1. Thank you.
2. Congratulations.
3. I'm sorry.
4. Heads up.

This I find is a good reminder of when communication should *not* be put off.

I SPREAD MY VENTURE CAPITAL WINGS

1994 was a critical year. Up until then, the shift in my assets had been all one way – from liquid securities, mostly publicly traded stocks like Coachman and Circuit City, to illiquid venture investments, most notably Advent Software on the plus side and my rocket dreams on the negative side. But in 1994, Advent Software went public. This began a six-year era (1994 to 2000) characterized by five successful round trips – venture investments that provided paydays: Advent Software (IPO) Information America (buyout); Best Internet (received publicly traded stock); OnPrem (received publicly traded stock); ValueClick (IPO).

My emotional reaction to this period included visualizing my speculative process as an assembly line – where I invested in start-ups at a low valuation and after two to four years saw my investment transformed into piles of cash. The assembly line was powered by the rise of the Internet. The growth of the Internet, the revolutionary state of its impact on life (email, websites, browsing, search, commerce, social media, etc.), fueled the biggest bubble in financial history. And I was riding it.

I saw that this necessitated fleshing out my strategy for speculating in the market of start-up venture capital. I was doing this as an individual investor. I knew I would be identified as an angel, a term I didn't like. I felt that most angels were nice amateurs, and I in contrast planned to be a gnarled, greedy professional. But how could I arrive at a strategy that as with other markets both worked and fit my personality?

CHAPTER SEVENTEEN

My Strategy for Venture Investing – Or Be Everything They Ain't

Every entrepreneur knows that most of the money invested in new ventures comes not from individuals or from existing companies but rather from venture capital firms (VCs). This is a recent phenomenon heavily fueled by the passage of the Steiger Amendment, which cut capital gains taxes in 1978. This tax cut fueled a massive rise in funding for VCs because it allowed them to promise their investors that gains made would be taxed at the new lower rate. A related feature was that the VC employees would also benefit because their cut of the gains (called carried interest) would also get the lower tax.

By the early 1990s, when I was developing my own venture investing strategy, VCs were the 800-pound gorillas in the minds of entrepreneurs. I would ask entrepreneurs I met if they looked to get VC funding. The most common answer I got was, "I hope not."

Why the reticence?

The image of VCs in the mind of the aspiring entrepreneur looking for money was – and is – far from totally positive. For one thing, it was difficult for most entrepreneurs to get a hearing from a VC. For another, even entrepreneurs who succeeded in getting a hearing where the VC expressed interest were shunted into a black hole of multiple meetings, demands for more information (what marketing studies have you done to determine the size of the market?), demands for increasing the team (you need some expert advisors on your board), etc., etc. – all before the VC would commit dollar one. And the few entrepreneurs who completed this marathon would have to wait a minimum of three months or more to get any investment. Additionally,

VCs liked to get as much control of the venture as they could either by insisting on buying a majority of the deal at the outset, often by insisting the entrepreneur take more money than they needed or wanted, or at a minimum putting in preferential terms into the contract (called a "term sheet") that many entrepreneurs, desperate to close the deal, agree to – to their later regret. The VCs felt such tactics protected their investment (and thereby fulfilled their fiduciary responsibility to protect their own investors), but the entrepreneur resented these same tactics.

This negative image of the VC in so many entrepreneurial minds led directly to how I speculate in venture capital. I would become the investor who would be the opposite of the VC.

The key tactic I developed to demonstrate how I was a different kind of VC was access. I would talk to any entrepreneur. Even better, I would schedule lunch with any entrepreneur. Better yet, I would always pay for lunch. This tactic had three critical pluses. First, anyone I met would think of me first – or at least early – if they heard of an intriguing deal looking for money. Second, by paying for lunch, I fostered the reputation of being generous. And third, I started the process of differentiating myself in the mind of the entrepreneur from the mainstream VC's negative image.

WINNOWING THE WHEAT FROM THE CHAFF

The key to *any* successful strategy in venture capital is answering this question: When you are analyzing a new speculation in venture capital, how do you decide which one to invest in?

The answer I came up with I call *the Four Ds*. I typically unleash the Four Ds early in that first meeting.

The first two Ds are the Dream and the Drive. The Dream means I want to hear from the entrepreneur why this new venture can become profitable quickly and cheaply. By far the best way to quick, cheap profits is to invest only in start-ups that in an important way are unique.

By the Drive, I mean I want at least one person to be dedicated – even driven – to building/leading the venture; that he or she is taking the entrepreneurial leap full-time, which is always far more than forty hours per week.

I remember that COMPAC was organized in Texas to build the IBM PC more cheaply, and it was a great success. Would I have ever invested in COMPAC? Absolutely not, because it was a "me too" idea and not sufficiently unique.

Note that from the beginning I planned to get into the venture capital business in a small way (i.e., without a lot of money), so I felt (and still do feel) that it is only by investing in something importantly unique that I had a chance of ending up with, to quote Dr. Johnson, "wealth beyond the dreams of avarice." This would be primarily because since the new venture was doing something unique, it was in effect creating and by definition dominating a *new* industry. And dominating a new industry meant avoiding getting all hot and sweaty competing with established players. Which normally meant running out of money.

And I finish my discourse of the first two Ds, the Dream and the Drive, by saying I don't know which is more important. I want them *both.*

And when the conversation gets to the point of my being satisfied about the first two Ds, then I reach into my pocket and slap my wallet onto the table and announce the third D: the Dough. I freely acknowledge that the Dough is less important than the first two. After all, there are many great companies that got going without outside money – Microsoft, Marriott, and Hewlett Packard, to name three. But there we are, and that's my turf in terms of getting this venture going.

"But," I continue, "I have seen many deals that had the Dream, the Drive, and the Dough in place but that never happened. Why?"

Because of the infamous fourth D: the Details – the lawyers, the accountants, the paperwork, and the relationships. Aunt Bertha can't stand Cousin Bertram, etc., etc.

"I have," I say, "two rules about the Details. First, Murphy's Law always applies: and second, if I want the Deal to happen, I have to just hover, focusing on bringing the Deal together. Maybe we got the wrong lawyer, maybe we have to sacrifice Cousin Bertram to satisfy Aunt Bertha . . . hover . . . hover . . ."

Until, finally, I can bring my hands together and announce, "The Deal is done."

One of the most important aspects of talking through the four Ds is that I am not industry specific. Unlike many venture investors, I from the beginning do not focus on an industry to invest in based on my knowledge of one industry, or for that matter my bias against another. Many investors like to invest in an industry they know. The successful software programmers like to invest in software start-ups; medical types like to invest in biotech, etc. But once I got seriously into speculating in venture – in 1993 – I was always open to hearing about anything . . . and that leads to the next aspect of my strategy.

FALLING IN LOVE

A key tactic that I learned from the venture capitalist and friend Jim Pelkey was the emotional state I want to be in when I hear about a new deal for the first time. Of the great stock market investors I have known, most, when listening to a new idea – whether a venture idea or a public stock to buy – are exercising their skeptical or even cynical side during that first conversation. But Jim does not, particularly when starting that first conversation with an entrepreneur about his venture. Instead, he tries to fall in love with the idea and the entrepreneur. And so do I. For example, if the entrepreneur with his mining engineering background wants to mine cheese on the moon, my first question might be, "Do you expect to mine more cheddar or more Limburger?" I further try to warm to the venture by making sure I hear of all the reasons the entrepreneur likes the deal. I also actively get creative and bring up any ideas that I think would enhance his deal.

Only after hearing the complete story will I start to exercise my skeptical side. Often this will happen in that first conversation if the deal is really bad, since I don't want to string people along – particularly entrepreneurs for whom the deal (and their use of time) is so much more important than it is for me. But if the deal snares even a chunk of my interest, then I don't get critical in that first conversation but keep trying to fall in love. And then that very night, I sleep on it. When I wake up in the morning, I review this new deal and ask myself the question, "How does investing in this deal make me feel?" Note that I give priority not to logic but once again to emotion. Should I feel uncomfortable or unsure about investing, then I zero in on what specifically concerns me and what questions I need to get the entrepreneur to answer.

I find the main advantage of trying to fall in love in the first conversation is that I can concentrate fully on what I am learning about the deal rather than bleeding off a major chunk of my mind in critiquing the pitch in real time. This contrasts with many investors I know, whose skeptical (or often cynical) monitor remains on 24/7.

MORE ON THE DOUGH: VALUATION BY THE NOVICE

I made two pioneering (for me) venture investments in 1983, one of which was Advent Software. Advent's CEO and co-founder (along with the great software architect, Steve Strand) was Stephanie DiMarco. At the time, both Stephanie and I were novices. She was a novice entrepreneur, and I was a novice venture capitalist.

One reason that Advent was such a success was the sparkling job Stephanie did raising money. When we got to negotiating terms (or as us VCs call it, "valuation"), I let her take control by suggesting a valuation. Even though I pushed for a better valuation, I then agreed to her counter.

I learned from that experience. Now any conversation I have with new entrepreneurs about valuation is very different.

MY VALUATION RANGE: $200,000 TO $2 MILLION

If all the entrepreneur has is his or her Dream and Drive, I will still value their contribution at no less than $200,000. I would typically want at least a 10 percent interest and no more than a 20 percent interest, which would translate into $25,000 to $50,000 for this first, or seed, round. The best way to keep the entrepreneurs' Drive at maximum levels is for them to get their first money and still have not only majority control of the venture but enough of a supermajority so that even when they raise a follow-on round of funding they will still maintain majority control.

On the other hand, I like to have at least a 5 percent interest – and preferably a 10 percent interest – so if the valuation is more than two million, it becomes more difficult to get the kind of humungous return of ten times or more that Greedy Bob inevitably is looking for.

Armed with my internal valuation range, I next need to find out what the entrepreneur's valuation ideas are. His ideas depend on whether he is unsophisticated or sophisticated.

A financially unsophisticated entrepreneur will either say, "Well, I talked to my friend/mentor/lawyer, who thinks I should get x percent for the money." Or, "I haven't done this before. What do you think?"

Here's how I answer the unsophisticated entrepreneur: "I will invest x amount of money at y valuation. I always insist that you not make a decision today but sleep on it and get back to me within, say, a week with your response." I typically email the entrepreneur my offer(s), by the way.

If the entrepreneur, when she gets back to me, counters with a higher valuation, then I respond, usually via email, with what I make clear is my final offer, which I hold open for no more than two weeks, after which it will expire.

If the entrepreneur does not take that offer, then I say something like "I understand and wish you well – feel free to contact me if things change."

The *sophisticated* entrepreneur, on the other hand, will typically have a business plan that he will smoothly flip open to show me how his valuation is justified as follows:

"As you can see, the projections in the business plan call for us to make x in year five and the company to be worth y at that time. The current valuation of z, which you would invest at, will give you a forty percent return on investment annually. Isn't that great!"

Here's how I answer the sophisticated entrepreneur.

"I understand," I say. "I have found there are two ways you can raise money: you can raise it at your valuation, and I understand why you think it is so valuable, or you can raise money fast. But you can't do both."

Then I counter with my offer, which is often dramatically below their number. And I ask – after they fall off the chair in horror – "How long have you been raising money?"

Normally they answer by saying they just started. Then I suggest that they keep looking but set a deadline – say two to three months – at which point, if they have not raised money, they will readjust their sights.

Much of the time I never hear from the entrepreneur again, but I remain open to hearing from them, and some of the best deals come together after such a hiatus.

Whenever I encounter an entrepreneur desperately worried about being out of money, I paraphrase Dr. Johnson's famous comment: "The prospect of being hung on the morrow wonderfully concentrates the mind."

CHAPTER EIGHTEEN

My Most Valuable Venture Valuation Tools – A Mosaic of Tactics

When I meet an entrepreneur with a deal I want to invest in but his/her price is too high, I go to work as follows:

TOOL NUMBER ONE: THE 90 PERCENT WHITTLE

My experience is that if this is a deal where they are trying to raise a lot of money (often because they have heard they should ask for a lot because mainstream VCs recommend it), I can whittle down the amount to be raised by 90 percent. The first tactic I employ is to shift the conversation as follows:

"So you wish to raise x amount of money. I don't want to invest that much. Instead, tell me: What is the smallest amount of money that would allow you to make real progress, and what is that progress?"

The best way to whittle down the amount of money is by whittling down the number of things they are trying to accomplish. Specifically, they need to focus more on fewer projects. For example, if they plan to introduce multiple products, then I ask them which single product they can get to market fastest and how much it would cost to just concentrate on that and delay everything else. I emphasize that getting something to market as fast and as cheaply as possible is good because you then get feedback from the market. My bias is that feedback from the market is more useful than spending money on projections or consultants. It is only the market of actual customers that can tell you what changes to make in the product, or even more important, when to scrap the initial product idea completely and shift to a different product (called in the VC game "the pivot").

This can result in the following: The entrepreneur wants to raise $2 million and give up 25 percent of the equity. Instead I offer to invest $200 thousand for 10 percent of the company. This is a win/win, since I have less money at risk and the entrepreneur can make important progress while giving up less dilution. I call this my *toe-in-the-water* strategy.

TOOL NUMBER TWO: SPEED

The typical mainstream VC takes three or more months after being introduced to a deal to invest. By contrast, I can get the job done in two weeks or less, which includes due diligence. To get money invested quickly, I will often make the first payment in the form of a convertible loan, so that the entrepreneur can get the money even before the lawyers have completed all the paperwork. Note how this works in the entrepreneurial mind. If the entrepreneur meets me wanting to raise $2 million and I whittle him down to $200,000 and then come in with a first payment of $25,000, I have his/her undivided attention on what I think could be a spectacular deal while risking only the toe in the water. Meanwhile, the mainstream VC competition is still deciding when to schedule a second meeting or what additional information they want the entrepreneur to provide.

TOOL NUMBER THREE: REFERRAL

I have invested in over fifty deals and have tried with every start-up CEO to earn the reputation of being easy and productive and honorable to work with. I have made good money in venture, meaning that there are a number of deals in which the CEOs have benefitted from my involvement. I always suggest to any entrepreneur to whom I have made an offer to have private one-on-one conversations with any of the CEOs that I have invested with, so the entrepreneur can learn what having me as an investor is like.

TOOL NUMBER FOUR: MY GREED

The typical entrepreneur looks at potential investors with a mixture of hope and nervousness. There is a base level of nervousness stemming from all the stories of how investors (including VCs) have out-maneuvered the entrepreneur via various legal and/or financial tricks. (Read *The First $20 Million is Always the Hardest* by Po Bronson.) This nervousness is typically increased if the investor talks in terms of trying to convince the entrepreneur how much he, the investor, wants to help; how much he is happy to be involved out of the goodness of his heart; how many resources that only he can provide; and so on.

By contrast, I will emphasize, "I am motivated primarily by my selfishness and greed – I am maneuvering to make the biggest return that I can. Which is why, if you and I come to a deal, I will insist that you have a lawyer, working for you, review the documents before you sign anything." If the entrepreneur doesn't have a lawyer, I have often offered to have my lawyer represent them with me paying the lawyer's bill. This requires my signing a letter to my lawyer freeing him from conflict of interest.

TOOL NUMBER FIVE: IT'S MY MONEY

Entrepreneurs find that there are two kinds of investors: those who say, "I am going to invest by bringing the money from my contacts/associates," and those who say, "I invest my own or my firm's money." I make sure the entrepreneur knows that I invest my own money. If the entrepreneur is talking to people and is not sure which kind of investors they are, I tell them to ask the other person, "Would you be investing your own money, or are you acting as an investment banker or finder in bringing in other money?"

Many people who claim to be investors are in actuality finders of money from other people, and usually only occasional finders. I tell entrepreneurs to be careful of such pretenders and not to pay them money upfront, nor to provide them with any form of exclusive on the deal. On the other hand, I advise entrepreneurs to be generous to those finders offering to work on commission or fulfillment only.

TOOL NUMBER SIX: THE GQ EFFECT

Occasionally, I come across an entrepreneur that has what I term the GQ (*Gentleman's Quarterly*) effect. This entrepreneur looks good, dresses well, is polished and speaks well, went to a top business school (usually Stanford or Harvard), and has a business plan that will present well to mainstream VCs and/or angels. I quickly advise the GQ entrepreneur to find another lead investor rather than me. Why?

Because they will have success in finding the money at a far higher valuation than I will want to pay. Therefore, I do them the courtesy of not wasting their time.

I look for an entrepreneur that does *not* have the GQ effect and therefore will be less likely to attract the big money but does ring my chimes (see the Four Ds).

TOOL NUMBER SEVEN: ALWAYS LEAVE THEM FRIENDLY

I typically am involved in multiple deals for start-ups in which I have not (yet) invested money but am happy to invest time. I offer my time in deals that I have not committed to invest in mostly to offer advice on how to improve their chances of raising money – for example, how to improve the business plan, or how to get the company going with less money (see TOOL NUMBER ONE), or utilizing my web of contacts to introduce them to additional resources/contacts they might need.

As a result, I believe almost every entrepreneur who has met me feels the time with me was not wasted. This positions me favorably should any of the people I meet end up hearing of another deal that needs money (an important source of deal flow). In contrast, many investors (including VCs) often burn up entrepreneurs' time and in the end provide no money. I always remember that time is the entrepreneur's most precious resource.

TOOL NUMBER EIGHT: GET THEM TO "NO"

I was told (I forget by whom) the following very good advice I usually give to entrepreneurs looking for money:

Once you (the entrepreneur) have given the potential investor information about your deal and he or she is somewhere in the "maybe" middle with their response – not "yes, I'll invest," not "no, I won't invest," but rather "maybe" – then you should ask a series of questions to see if you can get the investor to say no. Why? Because once you get the investor to say no, then the investor can no longer bleed more of your time, and you can move on to the next potential investor. This is particularly important when dealing with an investor who, for whatever reason, enjoys putting you through various hoops, such as: "I think you need to get more marketing data," or "I think your product should include x, so put together a proposal on how you would include x," or "I think you need to hire an expert in purchasing for your deal" and so on. A proper response on your part should be: "If I don't do this, are you going to invest?" And if the investor says no, then you can quickly wind up the conversation, thus saving yourself Lord knows how many hours of low-valued effort.

TOOL NUMBER NINE: TOP 10 PERCENT

Many start-up entrepreneurs are encouraged to find a high-profile board of directors. I warn entrepreneurs that most directors are more trouble than they are worth because they bleed time in the mistaken belief they are providing useful counsel. In my experience, if a director in a start-up provides the founder/CEO nothing useful but does manage to avoid bleeding anybody's time (including requiring no buttering-up), that director is in the top 10 percent of directors in the mind of the founder.

TOOL NUMBER TEN: THE BYZANTINE FORUM

Once I assembled a reasonable number of venture investments, I created the Byzantine Forum, which is a one-day conference in San Francisco. The format is to have morning sessions for the CEOs and other management of the companies to interact, which includes multiple sessions on common issues facing entrepreneurs. Then we have lunch, which is open for a small fee to investors and others. Typically, we have around 125 participants of which around one half are potential investors. I introduce each company who gives a two-minute "elevator pitch," which takes about an hour since we normally have around twenty-five presenting companies, most of which are looking for funding. Then, after lunch, we adjourn to an adjacent room set up with tables for each company providing random access to investors for the afternoon.

While some money is quickly raised for a few of the companies, I think the more important benefit of the Byzantine Forum is that a large number of ventures are introduced to a large number of potential investors. Networking is powerful.

Another benefit of the Byzantine Forum is that it allows me to give a consolation prize to entrepreneurs in start-ups I like but am not going to personally invest in. I invite such companies to the next Byzantine Forum.

CHAPTER NINETEEN
Venture Stumbles...and Recovers

I triage all deals. There are a few, but precious few, where the entrepreneurs are so spectacular that they take your seed investment and get to positive cash flow with nothing more. Stephanie DiMarco of Advent is an example. Lorenzo Maggiore of Skell, the maker of the Bug-a-Salt, is another. Then there are the deals that are going nowhere. In those, I lose the toe and walk away with a slight limp. But what about the group in the middle? Yes, they have run out of money, but they have made real progress and have real promise.

SO WE MADE THAT FIRST INVESTMENT AND THEY'VE RUN OUT OF MONEY: NOW WHAT?

The key questions with regard to this middle group are these:

- Do I still like the direction the venture is going, or is it time for a pivot – a major change in what product or service the venture intends to offer?
- How much more money is needed to get the venture to positive cash flow, either with their original product or the pivot?
- Do I have confidence in the founder remaining as CEO, or do we need to bring in a new CEO? Note that for the most part, if we do want to change the CEO, we tie that to the new investment. Having an operating partner like Mark Ludwig, who is capable of leading multiple ventures, is as invaluable as it is rare. But even if we are in a strong position to make a CEO change because we can link the new money to the new leader, the decision often involves office politics.

VENTURE OFFICE POLITICS

I can play office politics with ventures, and when pressed I am pretty good at it, even though I am on my non-operating lonesome.

During the 1990s, my major foray into office politics was at Best Internet. I was persuaded that the founding CEO had to change; I canvassed the board of directors one by one, and by the time I had assembled a majority of directors to go for a change, the current CEO (sniffing the wind) resigned on the spot. Bringing in another CEO was particularly contentious because the new CEO – coming over from a much larger company – needed an employment contract in place before he would agree, and the board of directors was uncertain. The fact that I was in a position to make a larger investment was crucial to my getting the change accomplished. Unfortunately, that new CEO over the next year bled too much of the company's limited cash in an expensive marketing program, resulting in Best descending into losses. But, fortunately, I continued my campaign of pleading with Jim Zarley to get involved. And once Jim did get involved, I immediately deferred all office political questions to him, as I detailed earlier.

And five years later, I teamed up with Mark Ludwig. Mark, with his management consulting background, is comfortable hovering over a number of our investments at once, including dealing with office politics as needed.

FOOLED BY INITIAL VENTURE SUCCESS: MY ROCKET MISTAKE

"It's not so much that I mind losing $250,000,000 in the auto industry, but I did think it would make a bigger splash."
~Henry J. Kaiser, 1954

1986 was a critical year. Because Advent Software was growing dramatically, I rationalized putting my successfully stock market speculative strategy on hold. Instead I allowed myself to get caught up in entering – wait for it – the rocket business. The *Challenger* disaster had triggered President Reagan's decision to "encourage the creation of a commercial space launch industry." I assumed my venture success with Advent meant I must know what I was doing in venture investing. And so I became the lead investor in not one but two rocket start-ups, one after the other, between 1986 and 1993. Because the amount of capital I put in – though significant to me – was a truly negligible amount for such a capital-intensive business, both companies I funded used the same strategy of seeking – and to their great credit getting – initial US Defense contracts to build and test new rocket engines. Though the CEOs of both companies worked hard, the final result was a total loss because:

- The start-ups I funded brought very little unique to the rocket business that could have differentiated them.
- I thought – wrongly – that my speculative success in the stock market could translate into finding others to invest along with me.
- I got swept up emotionally with getting into the business. Or, to put it another way: "You think you can enter the rocket business with an investment of only a few hundred thousand dollars? Are you crazy??"

WHAT I SALVAGED FROM THE ROCKET WRECK-AGE: MY REPUTATION

I did have one success in getting others to fund my rocket venture, but only by providing a personal guarantee for the bulk of the money. When the guarantee was called, some of my acquaintances recommended I refuse to pay, feeling that the guarantee could well be impossible to collect. I chose *not* to listen to them. Instead I sought and got an extension while I sought and eventually found a buyer for enough of my Advent Software stock to pay my obligation in full to my friend Tom Barry, who had provided the money from the Rockefeller venture fund he managed.

I believe that paying my obligation in full resulted in a significant and long-lasting surge in my ability to attract investors to subsequent venture deals. And it cemented my friendship with Tom Barry, who told me that many of those he knew in business would in my position have reneged on their obligation.

THE BIGGEST VENTURE SUCCESSES LEAD TO THE BIGGEST VENTURE MISTAKE

The Internet boom created the biggest bubble in my speculative lifetime. As the Internet was dawning, the stock market was already surging. By 1992, the market got to levels that in the past (over 2.5 times book value) had spelled trouble (read: 1929). And so I continued to stay clear of the stock market, even when Advent Software went public in 1994 and I was liquid again. I stayed out of the long side of the public stock market but instead reinvested the cash in my entry into the Internet boom – Best Internet. I rode the Internet bubble to five paydays from various venture investments by the market peak in 2000.

Blinded by my success in riding the bubble, I began to believe that my destiny as a speculator was to put money into start-ups or early-stage ventures and harvest at the other end paydays in the form of IPOs or buyouts. Therefore, I started to think when I got a payday, I should invest it not in liquid common stocks or (horror) in cash or bonds but instead find new venture investments (*very* illiquid) to make. This was in part because my hit ratio (percent of venture invest-ments that made money – mostly made *a lot* of money) was over 50 percent in the years from 1983 to 1998. So, in 1998, when I got a really big payday (Best Internet), I was ripe for the slaughter by any en-trepreneur who got my phone number.

I forgot the famous contrarian Humphrey Neill's warning: "Don't confuse brains with a bull market."

I listened intently (and foolishly) when my lawyers told me of the wrinkle that if I invested venture gains in new ventures quickly, I could postpone any taxes, state or federal.

This meme proved an illusion – essentially a perfect-storm illusion. I put large amounts of money into a number of inadequately researched start-ups because I felt I wanted to take advantage of the tax postpone-ment wrinkle, and while the tax postponement feature worked as far as federal taxes were concerned, the State of California burrowed into the origins of Best Internet, which ended up meaning I owed a huge chunk of cash. Also, I lacked a partner – someone whose start-up operating management expertise could help us both review which start-ups to invest in as well as provide those venture investments we did make with back-up management and/or management consulting experience (you *really* need both) as needed.

This left me vulnerable to the 2000 crash in the stock market, which particularly devastated the Internet stocks. I was left with negligible cash plus investments in a number of venture investments where the prospect of a near-term payday had vanished, along with the bull market.

I needed to maximize the chance that at least some of my venture investments would pay off. Could I personally provide the operating management to save my investments? Of course not. Instead, I had to rely on my top venture secret.

TOP VENTURE SECRET: RESILIENCE, THY NAME IS LUDWIG

During the bubble in 1998, since Jim Zarley was providing sustained excellent management for just one of my deals at a time (first Best and then ValueClick), I looked for someone else to prop up my lengthening list of venture speculations. I had the sense to call a school classmate named Mark Ludwig.

"I am long money," I told him. "I am long deals; I am short management. *Help!*"

To my great fortune, Mark agreed to become my operating partner.

What Mark brought more than anything was resilience. What do I mean by that? Before Mark's advent, if a start-up I was investing in ran into trouble, I essentially had no way of helping. My personality is that of a speculator, not an operator.

What, you ask, is the difference?

Let's say there are two people who have an investment in a start-up – one being (like me) a speculator and the other (like Mark Ludwig or Jim Zarley or Stephanie DiMarco) an operator. And we both hear of a major problem that has hit the company.

The operator thinks, *How can I solve the problem?*

The speculator thinks, *How do I cut my losses?*

See the difference?

Once Mark came aboard, he took a good look at all the private investments I had made, and in multiple cases he could help with major problems. Perhaps he could act as a management consultant for one deal, a part-time CFO in the second deal, take over as CEO in the third deal, and cut the losses by shutting down a fourth deal. And he further saved major bucks by convincing me to refrain from putting another dollar into several of our other investments.

A number of my venture investments were only saved by Mark's personal intervention.

Here are two examples:

AEROASTRO PART I

AeroAstro, founded in 1989, pioneered in designing and building small satellites at a dramatic fraction of the cost of satellites bought from major aerospace companies. Before Mark was involved, the company had already designed and built their first satellite, Alexis. A great and resounding success. But then came the actual launch and a great and very silent problem. Here is the story.

A Failure Called Alexis

"What we've got here is a failure to communicate."
~The Captain, *Cool Hand Luke*

Two brilliant aerospace engineers, Rick Fleeter and Richard Warner, founded AeroAstro (initially called Astronautics) to fulfill an order for a satellite for such a small amount of money ($3 million) that no existing satellite builder would touch it. The next smallest bid was $30 million – ten times what Rick as CEO was bidding. The order came from a scientist at Los Alamos National labs who had a limited budget for a satellite that would be a space telescope that, for the first time, looked into the X-ray spectrum rather than visible light. The scientist was desperate (tight on cash), and he knew of what Rick had done at Rick's previous aerospace company in SoCal. (Rick had saved a large satellite that had been put into too low an Earth orbit.) Rick envisioned an innovative method of using the satellite's remaining power to boost it into the appropriate orbit.

With the $3 million order in hand, the two aerospace engineers – Fleeter and Warner – founded the company in Rick's home outside Washington, DC. I came there to provide financial counsel when by chance they were getting aerospace advice from a key advisor, professor Dan DeBra, who had taught them both at Stanford. In the next two years, Rick and Richard not only designed and built Alexis, the world's first microsatellite and the world's first X-ray space telescope, but completed the project *under budget*, which meant for one-tenth of the price bid by the big aerospace companies.

And simultaneously, Rick found a rocket to carry Alexis into orbit. They picked a new rocket company – Orbital Sciences – that had a new rocket with space available (again at the right price) called the Pegasus. The Pegasus was a solid-fuel rocket that would come to play a part in the unfolding story.

It was then successfully launched into orbit using the Orbital Sciences' Pegasus. Great success all around, right?

Not at all. When AeroAstro sent a signal out to its satellite, it expected it to respond with the word "hello."

But instead, Alexis remained totally mute. It sent no communications back to Earth at all. Within days, Orbital Sciences promptly branded Alexis a failure and strongly implied it was AeroAstro's fault.

Alexis, said the aerospace press authoritatively, was a failure, and Rick and Richard's design flaws and overly cheap construction had to be to blame.

An ordinary satellite-building company might have accepted Orbital's conclusion and washed its hands of the seemingly doomed and useless satellite. But AeroAstro was no ordinary company. Day after day, week after week, Rick and Richard continued to try to get Alexis to respond to their signals, to get Alexis to say "hello."

And then one day, in response to the one thousandth inquiry, they heard:

"Hel . . ."

The message was short and was not repeated. But it turned Richard and Rick into full-time aerospace engineering detectives. What could cause Alexis, after such a long and total silence, to speak?

One theory was that the solar panels which generated the power to run Alexis had been damaged at the beginning of the launch process just after the airplane that had carried the Pegasus launch vehicle up into the atmosphere released it. As planned, the Pegasus then ignited its rocket engine and twisted radically to point up into space. Could that radical twist have been so violent as to have caused the damage to Alexis, keeping it almost, but not quite, silent? Our detectives focused on the position of Alexis in reference to the sun. If one and only one of the solar panels was operable, then the brief "Hel . . ." message could be explained by Alexis only now, by chance, pointing the remaining solar panel sufficiently toward the sun to generate a small amount of new power.

Rick and Richard gambled that if the trickle of new solar power continued, they could use it not to communicate but instead to point the solar panel more toward the sun, which could start pouring power into Alexis.

The gamble paid off!

As Alexis was repositioned, it came to life. And down from orbit came the first of a long series of gorgeous pictures of a universe never before seen. To see these images, Google "alexis telescope x-ray pictures."

AEROASTRO PART II: THE ADVENT OF MARK

But even though the wonderful success of Alexis triggered two new microsatellite orders, once those orders were completed, AeroAstro ran out of time to get more satellite orders. Revenues collapsed just as I convinced Mark Ludwig to come on board as my operating partner.

"Help," I said to my new partner. Immediately Mark dove into AeroAstro, taking the job of CFO, working with Rick, commuting to AeroAstro's offices in Herndon, VA, outside of Washington, DC.

How did Mark change AeroAstro?

The first step was a strategy session. AeroAstro had been a consulting group that bounced from one small satellite order to the next. But this was not a company. In order to become a company, AeroAstro needed to envision a long-term mission. All of the AeroAstro team, including, crucially, CEO Rick Fleeter, got on board with this change.

The next step was to create stable, permanent business structures, including both a sales force and an administrative function. Once again, getting everyone to buy in, including Rick, was crucial. Mark knew that a team that was as brilliant at aeronautical engineering often had difficulty giving respect and authority to professions like sales, marketing, and finance that know nothing about engineering. Mark, with his operating as well as consulting background, was able to achieve this buy-in.

Mark thinks the final major step was to find a real product with major potential that could be the core of the company's future. One reason for this was that few companies would pay much for a consulting group, since what they were paying for could walk out the door at any time. AeroAstro not only found as their key product a satellite sensing system called SENS but found in Globalstar a partner to help develop SENS.

Result? AeroAstro's revenues, which had dropped to under $1million in 1999, surged to over $10 million in six years. In 2006, the intrigue of SENS triggered a buyout of AeroAstro. Mark had turned an almost-certain venture loser into an important payday. Part of the proceeds I used to pay off the money I had borrowed to pay the California State income tax bite. *Whew!*

But as important a job Mark did in building value at AeroAstro, he did an even more valuable job for us both with another of the ventures that I had funded.

MEDSEEK

I got a call from Reece Duca's partner, Tim Bliss, in 1994. Tim's kids went to school with the kids of a local housewife who wanted funding for a start-up called MedSeek, to make websites for individual MDs. Tim asked if I would talk to her.

"Sure," I said, and shortly I flew down to Santa Barbara to meet Gale McCreary. This was right at the beginning of websites/webhosting, and I had learned that carving out a niche in the website-building business was a little like the Oklahoma land rush. If you were the first to rush into an unclaimed territory, you had a chance of making it. Nobody was focused on websites for MDs, and since there were several hundred thousand MDs, it had big potential. I decided to invest. I had been seeing at Best Internet how quickly websites were growing. I also liked that Gale and her business partner, the website designer David Ross, would be totally focused on MedSeek. And I could get a good deal on valuation, since there were no other investors beating down Gale's door.

And so I invested and the company started marketing to MDs . . .

After three months, no more than five MDs had ordered at the $500 price. What was going wrong? Well, Gale would set up a meeting with an MD and explain how useful a website could be, and the MD would express some level of interest but hardly ever follow through. Many of the MDs worried that a website with information they were responsible for could possibly lead to lawsuits from unhappy patients.

Downer . . .

As Gale and I talked over the disappointing sales results, she brought up a new idea.

"Bob, what if we built a website for free for a local Santa Barbara hospital? This could show people what MedSeek could do – and I am having trouble getting much revenue from individual MDs. Maybe hospitals could be an easier sell than individual MDs."

"Good idea," I responded. "Go for it."

Shortly, the website was complete and up on the web for anyone to see. And someone had seen it and wanted to sell it to hospitals – an elite athlete who had never sold anything, let alone a complicated website. Why did he want to sell it? Because he was a professional tennis player with sore knees.

I made a call to Traverse City, Michigan. Mark Ludwig could not be involved full time because Mark was CEO and founding partner of another of my investments, the profitable welding firm TriMet. But Mark did agree to act as a management consultant to MedSeek.

What did Mark do first?

He got the tennis player, Peter Kuhn, to agree to work for commission only – no salary – by giving him a massive commission: 30 percent of revenues in the first year. But David Ross could build hospital websites so efficiently MedSeek could pay the 30 percent and laugh all the way to the bank.

He agreed to fly to Birmingham, Alabama, to meet Peter, who was to set up interviews with three hospital prospects.

He provided the Ludwig touch on how to help Peter cross the infinite leap from zero customers to one by deploying a secret weapon, the *Puppy Dog Sale*:

> A six-year-old boy is walking with his parents past a pet store with a puppy in the window.
>
> "Oh, Daddy, can I see the puppy?"
>
> So into the store they go, where the boy and puppy leap toward each other in joyous tail wagging, face licking, petting, and instant bonding.
>
> In the store, the owner informs the parents that the puppy is an expensive purebred, allowing the father (or so he thinks) to inform his son that they can't afford the puppy.
>
> "But," the owner continues, "why don't you take the puppy home for the weekend – no charge. Bring it back Monday if you decide not to buy it."
>
> "OK," says the father.
>
> And don't you know that on Monday, the father comes to the store not to return the puppy but rather to conclude the *Puppy Dog Sale*.

When Mark arrived at the Birmingham airport, did everything go smoothly? Not exactly. Peter, despite his diligent calls, could find only one hospital willing to talk. Worse, Mark and Peter were informed that the hospital CEO had a nephew ready and willing to design the website. Once the meeting started, Mark offered to have MedSeek design a website on spec, in competition with the CEO's nephew.

A few days later, Gale and Peter called Mark. "Mark, we didn't get the deal, but we really appreciate the progress on improving Peter's selling skills."

"Stop," Mark replied. "Nobody turns down my Puppy Dog Sale! What's her phone number?"

"Look," Mark explained to the hospital administrator, "MedSeek will complete the website design before your CEO's nephew, Billy Bob, can find his way to the men's room. On top of that, you can check out your new website for thirty days and then return it if you don't want to pay our $5K bill. You've got nothing to lose."

"Well, OK, if you put it like that..."

Five weeks later, the $5K check arrived and MedSeek's surge began.

MEDSEEK EQUITY TO KIRK

When I asked Mark Ludwig to consult with the MedSeek start-up, I had a lot of flexibility on how to make his engagement work best. A key aspect was TriMet. If Mark was going to be spending considerable time helping MedSeek, what would that do to the prospects of TriMet, where his partner, Kirk Schuch, had relied on Mark's full-time focus?

Nothing good.

My overriding rule on doing business deals is that I want to be able to walk down any street in any town and not care who I see coming the other way. Specifically, if Kirk Schuch came walking down the street, I didn't want him to say, "Gee, Bob, I see you sold MedSeek for megabucks, but because you took Mark's effort away from me, TriMet has gone under. Thanks a lot!"

So the deal I did regarding MedSeek equity in 1994 was to provide Mark with a 5 percent ownership in MedSeek, but a quarter of that 5 percent, or 1¼ percent, would go directly to Kirk.

Mark tells me that eighteen years later, when MedSeek was sold, he enjoyed telling Kirk how much cash he would get for his MedSeek stock, and Kirk's wife was able to get, among other things, the new garage in their Traverse City home.

MARK IN ACTION: TWO DILEMMAS OF QUALITY CONTROL

In 1970, right out of business school, Mark worked as the assistant to the CEO of a microchip company. The company was betting the store on developing a new chip. The chip designers were delighted with the new chip they had developed, but the chip manufacturing division was not happy. Too many chips failed the quality control system.

Was it the fault of the chip design? How about the manufacturing process? Fingers were pointed; voices were raised. Finally, the frustrated CEO asked Mark for help. And Mark found the answer that no one else could come up with. If the design is solid and the manufacturing process is too, then let's check to see if the quality control process itself is flawed. And so it proved to be. Mark heroic; company saved.

In 1980, Mark was called in to become CEO of a military truck grill supplier to the Pentagon. It was desperation city because the company was behind in supplying a new grill, and the lack of grills that met the Pentagon's quality standards was holding up the delivery of the trucks. Not good. Mark immediately started the process of turning the company around by refocusing the team on ramping up both quantity and quality. Soon the quantity of finished grills began to mount. Mark's management was working. *Until . . .*

The Pentagon quality control expert showed up to evaluate the first 200 grills ready to be shipped. Mark was in his office when he was informed that the quality control expert had rejected one of the grills. Mark got up and walked through the plant. He picked up a two-by-four on the way. On arriving, he noticed the Pentagon expert had several of the grills lined up for inspection. Right-handed Mark loudly slapped the two-by-four against his left hand. He asked which of the grills was rejected, and the Pentagon expert pointed to the first in a row.

CRUNCH! Mark smashed the grill to smithereens. Then Mark pointed to the next grill in line. "How's that grill?" Mark asked the Pentagon expert, again slapping the two-by-four against his other hand.

The Pentagon expert paused and finally lowered his eyes. "That passes," he said.

Mark pointed his two-by-four at the next grill in line. "How about that one?"

"That passes too."

"Let me know if there are any other rejections," he said and turned back to his office. Later that day, Mark was informed that the company was cleared to ship 199 grills.

MARK AND TRIPLING

Mark, from his consulting days, has a framework for the kinds of problems he is likely to have to deal with as a company grows. His experience is that companies up to $1 million in revenues are small enough that one key entrepreneur can cover all the bases and make all needed decisions. But when a company moves above one million up to three million, two major changes are vital. First, the entrepreneur has to delegate important chunks of the business to others – it's now too big to be a successful one-man band. And second, the delegation has to be accompanied with more attention to systems. The larger company needs a comprehensive series of standard rules for dealing with common problems that are understood by the team. When the company grows beyond $3 million on the way to $10 million, now the entrepreneur has to delegate not merely functions (like who is going to be the CFO) but management, since most of the team will no longer report directly to her or him.

We have had a great advantage in our venture speculations by Mark using his tripling framework to zero in on what needs to be done.

VALUECLICK: FROM GALE TO BRIAN TO $ TO JIM

In 1995, shortly after MedSeek had surged into profitability, I got a call from Gale McCreary. She had hired an Internet advertising consultant named Brian Coryat. Brian had started on the side a new venture called ValueClick that specialized in selling banner ad space for small websites to advertisers and splitting the revenue. ValueClick was growing dramatically, but Brian, bootstrapping ValueClick totally, was running out of money.

"Why not find an investor for ValueClick?" Gale asked.

"Do you know anyone who might invest?"

And so, after Gale's call, I went down to Santa Barbara to meet Brian and ValueClick. I was instantly excited by the dramatic sales growth and massive potential of the company. Brian and I shook hands on a deal, and within days I had tapped my credit cards to the tune of $50,000 to become ValueClick's first investor. And then what did I do? I had Brian come up to the offices of Best Internet to meet Jim Zarley.

Within months, Jim and I had put together a business plan that raised $2,000,000 by featuring the company's dramatic growth and the partnership of Brian Coryat's entrepreneurial vision and Jim Zarley's management power.

Of course, part of the success of my foray into ValueClick came from being early in the Internet cycle, but the tactics I was developing for speculating in venture didn't hurt either.

DURING THE GOOD TIMES: THE INTERNET BUBBLE

The comparative ease of making money by investing in the multiple burgeoning niches of the Internet lasted for only six years, 1995–2000. One reason it was so easy to make money was that one could fund a start-up that, long before it became profitable, could be bought out at a major profit if it could demonstrate progress (termed *milestones*) in capturing some Internet niche. Here are three examples:

I invested in OnPrem, a start-up dedicated to providing apartment house landlords a way to sell Internet access to individual apartment renters. Once we found a couple of VCs to invest in a second round of funding, Copper Mountain, a publicly traded company, not waiting to see if OnPrem could actually launch a product, swooped in and bought out OnPrem, providing us early investors with a several-fold return in only two years. Wow!

Meanwhile, up until 2000, ValueClick grew dramatically by consolidating the banner ads of a large number of small websites. This provided an efficient way for advertisers to spread their Internet advertising budget. But once the Internet boom collapsed in late 2000, ValueClick revenues declined because a major portion of the advertisers were themselves unprofitable start-ups spending their VC investors' money, which was now harder to get. This illustrates how pervasive were the twin illusions that to succeed in the Internet meant you had to get big fast, and that growth in traffic to a website meant the value of the venture was increasing, even if it was showing major losses. Jim Zarley told me that his having to cut expenses and employment on three separate occasions during the 2000–2002 down period was the most difficult challenge of his career, but without those cuts, ValueClick would not have survived.

And at MedSeek, often our hospital clients wanted new features for the websites we were designing for them and expected MedSeek to pay for those features up front as some of MedSeek's competitors agreed to do. But instead, taking Mark Ludwig's advice, Gale was adamant on charging the customers for the cost of developing new features. As a result, MedSeek also survived the Internet downturn in 2000.

CHAPTER TWENTY

The Internet Changes Almost Everything – But Not Human Nature

As I am finishing this book, one recent investment illustrates that some things change (bowing most deeply to the Internet), but some don't. I find the main difference in speculating after the Internet, versus before it, is that it's now much easier to get and transmit information. But human nature has not changed. This means the opportunities to find successful speculative investments still abound. Consider the following example.

START-UP VENTURE CAPITAL: BOUSTEAD

In 2012, I had a major payday with the sale of hospital Internet website leader MedSeek. This allowed me to invest a chunk into a small investment banking firm called Monarch Bay. Why make this investment? Because it gave me a chance to partner with one of the most important weapons in my stock market forays – the stock trader Thad Mercer. Thad's new firm was run by two partners who together owned a majority of the company and had worked together for years. Alas, the first three years after I invested were a pretty grim spiral to bankruptcy. Although only one of the two partners, the CEO, was making bad and costly decisions, as long as he got support from the other partner, the CFO, Thad and I were powerless to make any change.

I remained mellow, as I had learned from Dr. Morter and B.E.S.T. to spend little time worrying about things I couldn't change. Inevitably, the day came when the CFO, Keith Moore, told Thad that Monarch

Bay had burned through almost all my money. Thad called me. It was time, I thought, for venture office politics, once again quoting Dr. Johnson: "The prospect of being hung on the morrow wonderfully concentrates the mind." And (paraphrasing) Shakespeare: "If it were done, 'tis best were done *quickly*."

The next week, after I flew down to LA and pounded, as needed, my fist on the table, Keith Moore was promoted from CFO to CEO. The sigh of relief was palpable. I did my normal tactic of being in the top 10 percent of directors by leaving Keith alone other than providing (with Thad's help) just enough additional money to keep the doors open during the following year's difficult industry conditions. The result? Keith turned the company around, merged with the more seasoned (founded in 1828) Boustead Securities, and made Boustead into one of Thad's and my major venture successes as an innovative "one-stop middle-market investment bank" specializing in smaller initial public offerings (IPOs).

As 2019 progresses, Boustead continues to make such progress that to be honest, I've felt the same upwelling of greed that I first felt in 1975 when Bill Griswold warned me to not buy Coachman. Therefore, I conclude that my old standbys – emotion, illusion, and where we are in the (industry) cycle – are still present and germane to the market. In short, human nature still rules. And those readers who use my tactics still have the opportunity to profit.

Go for it!

CHAPTER TWENTY-ONE

Summarizing My Venture Capital Investing Strategy

The collapse of the Internet bubble in 2000 had a profound impact on my venture capital results. The paydays stopped with a jolt. The ValueClick IPO payday was short-circuited because I was locked up as an insider (director), and by the time the lockup expired, the stock was down over 80 percent. A related problem was that I had, in 1998, invested carelessly into a series of early-stage ventures and, as a result, had massively drained the liquidity I had almost causally garnered during the Internet boom years.

Mark and I had to adjust our strategy. At Mark's initiation, we split prospective investments into two categories – venture investments made strictly for financial gain on the one hand, and investments tied to my personal charitable impulse on the other. All venture investments, whether new or follow-on, required Mark's approval.

In the period since 2002, our speculations in venture capital have been increasingly successful. I measure this success not so much in terms of how much money I made. I made the most money riding the Internet boom of the 1994–2000 bubble. Rather, I measure success by considering the high percentage of the invested money going into deals that became profitable. The key to this success involves the following seven strategies:

1. Investing only in deals that satisfied the four Ds, with particular focus on uncovering an entrepreneur of high dedication to a dream that has an important element of uniqueness. (Put another way, is the new venture in an important way seeking to do something that no one else was doing?)

2. Positioning myself in opposition to the mainstream VCs by

focusing on start-ups with entrepreneurs without the GQ effect.

3.   Using the *toe-in-the-water* tactic.
4.   Only considering deals with the prospect of getting to profitability with an austere investment capacity (seldom investing more than $500,000 in any new deal) that I could stomach.
5.   Investing only my own money. This means that I stick to start-ups or very early-stage investing. This is where the relatively small amount of money I can afford to invest can have the biggest impact.
6.   Having every entrepreneur leaving a meeting thinking, "Meeting Bob Leppo was a good use of my time."
7.   Partnering with Mark Ludwig, whose unique combined mastery of consulting and turnaround management were invaluable. Mark's comfort in working with deals spiraling toward bankruptcy matches my comfort in dealing with an investment portfolio spiraling toward illiquidity.

This period of success commenced in 2002. Already the number of new deals we invested in had shrunken markedly. I cut back on my personal burn rate, which emotionally I have no problem with, as I once again confirmed what Dr. Johnson had noticed in the eighteenth century: "The prospect of being hung on the morrow wonderfully concentrates the mind."

But even though I have had overall speculative success, I still made important mistakes. It's worth looking at how you, the reader and presumably budding speculator, can do better than I have done.

HOW CAN YOU USE MY TOOLS TO DO BETTER THAN I DID

I do have a few flaws. I offer this list in hopes that you will be able to learn from mine and avoid them.

1.   Complacency. In liquid markets – I'm talking about both the stock market and commodity futures trading – my tendency is that when a speculation goes my way, I get complacent and do not do a disciplined job of deciding whether I should get out of winning plays now that they have realized a lot of the promise. It is true that I put together a system of tables for evaluating alternative investments, which pushed me to

switch out of investments that had become less attractive in favor of other alternatives. But the complacency combined with over-laziness allowed me to let those tables slide. Just as important in trading futures, I did not put in new stops to preserve a profit nearly as often as I should have.

2.   Laziness. A related flaw is that I am lazy. As time has gone by, I am less disciplined in getting complete information before making a move, particularly when most of my assets are in illiquid venture deals. This allows me to rationalize my lack of discipline by thinking my life is not going to change much even if I make a mistake in a liquid position due to laziness.

3.   Tendency to overemphasize the price-to-book metric for the stock market. In 1990, the price-to-book value of the stock market moved up to historic highs (surging above 2.5 to 1). I concluded that I needed to pull out of speculating in the American stock market in general . . . and this blunder caused me to miss a huge opportunity in the year 2000. I bought gold and silver futures, thinking rightly that gold and silver prices were due for a major rally. But because I was out of the stock market, I missed a glaringly obvious way to use the stock market to play the rise in gold and silver prices – so I missed the truly mammoth gains I could have garnered by investing in gold and silver mining stocks.

4.   Rationalizing how my hearing loss affected how I speculated. In the early 1980s, my hearing had deteriorated to the point where I stopped visiting companies because it was difficult to understand conversations. This tied into why I got out of the stock market in 1990. So, when I received my first major venture capital payday – Advent Software going public in 1993 – I failed to restart my research into individual stocks.

CHAPTER TWENTY-TWO

Conclusion: The Mosaic of Speculation

There is no conclusion.

> "It's got to be the going, not the getting there that's good."
> ~Harry Chapin

> "The journey is the reward."
> ~Steve Jobs

I actively speculate in three markets: the US stock market, the commodity futures market, and the US-based start-up venture capital market. In all three, the tactics that I have found most useful are based on emotion, illusion, and cyclicality.

All of my successful speculations begin by looking to bet against the illusions that ensnare the mass of investors. But since the power of any illusion is cyclical, timing the bets for maximum gain is tricky and often frustrating. I have personally grown most emotionally comfortable with using the collapse of a bubble to time getting into a common stock or commodity speculation. And I have personally grown emotionally most comfortable with investing in venture start-ups doing something truly unique.

The best chance of success comes to those who understand their own emotions and love what they do. Someone who loves speculation loves:

- The thrill of competing against others.
- Gambling in and of itself.
- The sustained avoidance of the heavy lifting required to actually build something by finding partners who love the

building.

Once you make enough to live on, finding a long-term incentive for continuing to speculate is a good thing. That incentive should be something that allows you, when you get up in the morning, to look at yourself in the bathroom mirror and like who you see.

About the Author

Born in Baltimore in 1943, Robert Leppo moved west at the age of four with his mother and older brother on the death of his father Arthur Deute. To his good fortune, when Bob was five, his mother married Harrison Leppo, who as a San Francisco investment counselor had much to teach Bob in his early years. An early obsession with reading allowed Bob to dive into history and geography and the biographies of great tycoons like Andrew Carnegie, great speculators like Jesse Livermore, and great empires like Byzantium.

This book chronicles how Bob was able to combine a major dose of the gambling instinct, initially cultivated in poker, with an ability to learn from his many mistakes to fuel a successful, if volatile, career as a private investor focused at various times on three markets: the US stock market, the commodity futures market, and the start-up venture capital market. Bob lives in San Francisco.

Made in the USA
Las Vegas, NV
16 March 2022

45773402R00090